LIFE IN AN INDIAN VILLAGE

LIFE IN AN INDIAN VILLAGE

T. RAMAKRISHNA, B. A.

GYAN

Published by

GYAN

Gyan Publishing House
5, Ansari Road
Daryaganj, New Delhi-110002
Phone: 011-47034999, 9811692060
E-mail: books@gyanbooks.com

Distribution Network
gyanbooks.com
India, USA, Canada, UK, Australia, France

ISBN: 978-81-212-8610-7 (PB)
First Published, 1891

2nd Impression 2023

Printed at: Gyan Press, Delhi.

LIFE IN AN INDIAN VILLAGE
Author: T. Ramakrishna

LIFE IN AN INDIAN VILLAGE

LIFE IN AN INDIAN VILLAGE

BY

T. RAMAKRISHNA, B.A.

WITH AN INTRODUCTION BY

THE RIGHT HONOURABLE

SIR M. E. GRANT DUFF, G.C.S.I.

London

T. FISHER UNWIN

PATERNOSTER SQUARE

MDCCCXCI

CONTENTS.

CHAPTER I.

CHAPTER II.

CHAPTER III.

CHAPTER IV.

PAGE

CHAPTER XI.

CHAPTER XII.

CHAPTER XIII.

CHAPTER XIV.

CHAPTER XV.

INTRODUCTION.

I HAVE been asked by Mr. T. Ramakrishna, the writer of these sketches, which appeared originally in a magazine published at Madras, to put a preface to them in their collected form. I am very willing to do so, because the little book appears to me an honest and intelligent attempt to convey to the English public some ideas about the life led by ninety per cent. of the people in the most Indian part of India.

In the north of that country or continent, one invasion after another, from the far-off coming of the Aryans all through history, has profoundly modified the conditions of life. The vast Dravidian population of the South itself probably came to India from outside, but so long ago that no one can say either whence it started or when it established itself in its present seat.

Europeans, despairing perhaps of finding out much about its ancient history, have very generally neglected it. All the more desirable is it that Dravidians who have been educated in our schools and colleges should devote themselves to inquiries relating either to the present or the past of their own people.

The author of the sketches takes a village of some fifty or sixty houses which he considers to be a typical representative of some fifty-five thousand such villages scattered over the Madras Presidency, a province considerably larger than the British Isles. He describes it as situated on the Palar between Conjeeveram and Mahabalipuram, which is not far from the spot best known to Europeans as "the Seven Pagodas" made famous by Southey's "Curse of Kehama." To his village he gives the real or imaginary name of Kélambakam. I never saw it, but many is the place just like it which I have seen. He describes it as:

"A cluster of trees, consisting of the tamarind, mango, cocoanut, plantain, and other useful Indian trees; a group of dwellings, some thatched and some tiled; a small temple in the centre—these surrounded on all sides by about five hundred acres of green fields, and a large tank capable of watering these five hundred acres of land for about six months."

He then proceeds to pass in review with full particulars—but, I presume, under fictitious names—all the leading personages of the little community.

First, of course, comes the village headman, or village *Munsiff* as he is commonly called.

Secondly, the public accountant or *Kurnam.*

Thirdly, the policeman, and

Fourthly, the Brahmin sage.

These are followed by the schoolmaster, the *Vythian* or physician, the carpenter, the blacksmith, the shepherd, the washerman, the potter, the barber and his wife.

The centre of the religion of Kélambakam is the temple of the local goddess Angalammal, which stands a furlong or two from the rest of the houses; and she has, of course, her priest or *Pujari*, under whom are various servants of the shrine, with which are also connected a couple of dancing girls.

Then we have the *Panisiva*, a sort of general servant of the village; next the money-lender, the local banker, the description of whom recalls the observation which I once heard made by a botanical guide in the south of France, who was not aware that he was addressing one of the most dignified of the potentates of Lombard Street: "Mais vous savez, Monsieur, ces banquiers sont toujours Juifs!"

Lastly are enumerated the humblest personages in the local hierarchy—the tanner, to whose occupation, in a land where the cow is sacred, great discredit naturally attaches; the tattooer, the *Villee*, who gathers, and exchanges for grain, honey, roots, medicinal herbs, and other forest produce. Add to these a small community of pariahs (who live in a little quarter of their own and were formerly in the position of serfs, but to whom the author of this work gives an excellent character), and the little microcosm is complete.

"It will be seen," says Mr. T. Ramakrishna, "that this village is a little world in itself, having a government of its own and preserving intact the traditions of the past in spite of the influences of a foreign government and a foreign civilization. Every member of the little state of Kélambakam regularly performs the duties allotted to him, and everything works like a machine. Those that render service for the upkeep of the village constitution are either paid in grain or have some lands allotted to them to be cultivated and enjoyed free of rent. Those that are paid in grain present themselves during the harvest time at the threshing floor; and when the villager gathers his corn and is ready to remove it to his house, he distributes a portion to each of the village servants, according to the nature and importance of the service rendered to him throughout the whole year. And these simple, honest villagers earn their livelihood, year after year, by toiling hard from early morning till close of day, leading a peaceful and contented life, living happily with their wives and children in their humble cottage homes, and caring for nothing that goes on beyond their own little village."

Nor are they without amusements which bring them often together, and we have detailed to us the gossip of the women when they congregate to draw water; we are allowed to witness the delight with which the village bards are listened to, as well as to watch the performances of the jugglers, of the acrobats, of the snake-charmers, and of the animal-tamers. Some of the feats of these people have been frequently described by Europeans in India, but I never happened to hear of anything like the doings of the bull Rama and the cow Seeta which will be found in the text, and are, I dare say, very correctly recounted.

Chapter XI. contains a long sermon, on a portion of the Mahabaratha, which purports to have been delivered by the village schoolmaster; while Chapter XII. is given up to an account of a village drama. The Thirteenth is devoted to feasts and festivities, while the Fourteenth, a particularly interesting one, treats of the doings of a religious confraternity.

In a very brief but excellent concluding chapter, Mr. T. Ramakrishna makes a few reflections upon the most noticeable features of Indian village life.

"The first is," he says, "the extreme importance attached to religion. Every other thing gives way to this important aspect of Hindu life. In religion the Hindu lives, moves, and has his being. His whole action, his whole thought, all that he does day by day, and on occasions of marriages and funeral ceremonies, is tinged with religion. The one pervading idea with the Hindu is how to get rid of future births and obtain eternal beatitude. We have seen how in dramatic performances gods are introduced to bless a truthful and honest man, how educated animals are trained to act the parts of Rama, Lakshmana, and Sita, and how in popular tales recited in Hindu homes the religious element is largely introduced. We thus find religion to be the foundation of everything Hindu. The very construction of an Indian village bears ample evidence to this fact. A temple is built and dedicated to the deity worshipped, and round the temple a village springs up. It is a rare phenomenon in India, at least in Southern India, to find a village without a temple. The religious Hindu will not settle down in a village where there is no temple, and where, accordingly, he has no chances of acquiring religious merit!"

The second feature is the immense importance attached to water. The third is the mutual service system, which still exists in full force in the midst of a world in which money has become so important that people often forget that it is nothing more than the measure of services.

The two chief objects of Mr. T. Ramakrishna's aversion—I might say the only ones, for he is a most amiable critic—are the village money-lender and the pettifogging lawyer. For the one he would substitute agricultural banks, while the other he would drive out by recalling into constant action the old village *Panchayet*, or council of five. By all means let this last be done in so far as it is possible; but as long as in all suits there is a successful and an unsuccessful party, it is to be feared that the unsuccessful party will not be satisfied without appealing to a higher tribunal, often no doubt to the wasting of his own substance as well as that of the other litigant.

As for agricultural banks, it would no doubt be an excellent thing if they could be established; and often and often has the suggestion been made, but the practical difficulties are very great. If this were not so, we should have seen them tried on a large scale long ere this.

It is not sufficiently remembered that

the village money-lender is only able to demand and to obtain an immense interest because he has often to lend on very miserable security. How far could governmental institutions or powerful corporations of capitalists fulfil the same function as he without incurring the same unpopularity, and doing a thousand things which could be plausibly represented as extremely harsh, not to say atrocious?

The abuses of the present system are certainly great; but as the people become more acquainted with the elementary arts of reading, writing, and arithmetic, some of these will disappear, and the day may dawn when, without any state-intervention, banks may be as common in India and as useful in the development of the country as they have long been in Scotland.

I think the reader of this work will carry away a pleasant, as I am sure he will carry away a correct, general impression of the character of the people of Southern India. He will see that no good can be effected for them, but only much harm, by introducing European methods of government, foreign alike to their characters and conditions. What we can do, and what, thank God, we have been doing now for several generations, is to enable these myriad little worlds to live in peace instead of being, as they were before our time, perpetually liable to be harried and destroyed by every robber or petty tyrant who could pay a handful of scoundrels to follow him.

In Tinnevelly, the southern district of the Madras Presidency—far from being one of the wildest, when the civilians who have just retired after the end of their service were entering upon it, there was a gang-robbery—that is, burglary diversified with murder and torture, every night of the year. I had occasion shortly before leaving Madras to ask the head of the police, how many gang-robberies there had been in that district in the previous year. His answer was, "Not one."

"Hae tibi erunt artes."

These are the things which it is worth her sons leaving these far Atlantic islands to do at the ends of the earth!

We can benefit and are benefiting the Indian villager by improving his water supply, by preventing his wells being polluted, by encouraging the growth of forest around the head-waters of his rivers, and by so connecting the tank or artificial lake which irrigates his field with the general irrigation system of the country as to make it as little likely to dry up as may be.

Then if there comes, as come there assuredly will, several seasons together when the rainfall is inadequate, we can bring food to his door by road and railway instead of allowing him to starve in his isolation as did, from time to time, all his fathers for some thousand years.

We can see that the village headman dispenses justice fairly. We can see that the village accountant does not rob; we can see that the village policeman is not oppressive; we can give the schoolmaster something sensible to teach; we can make the Vythians—who although their name comes from the same root as Video, "I see," know much less than nothing, because their minds are filled with every kind of nonsense—possess at least the rudiments of medicine, and we can dot the country over with good surgeons and with midwives who are acquainted with a thousand secrets of nature unknown to the barber and his spouse.

We can introduce new products and create new industries while we improve old ones; we can teach the villager how to combat his deadliest enemy, fever, as Mr. Marmaduke Lawson is so well doing at this very moment; we can enable him to circumvent small-pox, as Mr. Forster Webster did in Tanjore, and as the great goddess Mariamma, in spite of many prayers, never has done. We can teach him how to keep his streets and his back-yards in a sanitary condition; we can greatly improve his agriculture, we can give him better breeds of cattle; and when a youth of real ability shows himself amongst his sons, we can educate him till he, in his turn, becomes a useful member of the administration or finds his place as an active merchant, an intelligent farmer, or a worker in some one of the many careers which stand open to native merit.

It is a too prevalent idea in England that our system does not afford many openings to native merit in the service of Government. There could not be a greater mistake. Of course the work of *supervision* in the higher places of the administration must, for the most part, remain in European hands. That stands to reason; but it would probably not be an exaggerated estimate to say that for every European employed in the southern province of India there are well on to fifty natives, while every one who has administered the patronage of that country knows that he has often hungered and thirsted for properly qualified natives to promote in certain departments of the official hierarchy, without being able to find what he desired.

Our service, sooth to say, attracts an undue proportion of the intelligence of the country. The sweets of official life and the prizes of the Bar are such that they tend to starve other professions, and above all those which Southern India probably most wants at this moment, the medical and the agricultural professions.

These are the two which in the interest of the Indian villager I should most like to see grow and prosper.

While we merely raise candidates for Government employment and for the contentions of the law court, we run great danger of creating an educated proletariat, one of the worst curses that can afflict any country.

To discuss that subject would, however, take me too far from the Indian village, and I willingly hand over the reader to the excellent guidance of the native gentleman who is ready to direct his steps on the banks of the Palar.

M. E. GRANT DUFF.

I.

Introductory remarks—The headman—The accountant—The watchman

"HAS any one studied the village life of the South? Are there no facts to be collected from a careful examination of it, which would be useful to some future Sir Henry Maine? If there are, surely you should be the people to collect them. It makes one who has a strong feeling for South India a little sad, to read such a book as Professor Max Müller's *India, What can it teach us?* and to see how very little it has to do with India south of the Vindhyan range." So said our late Governor, Sir M. E. Grant Duff, in the remarkable address he delivered last year to the Madras University graduates, when, in his capacity of Chancellor of the University, he drew their attention to the several branches of study to which they could usefully devote their time and in which they might instruct their Aryan brother of the West. Life in an Indian village is a very interesting study, and it is the object of the present book to picture the life of the Hindu as seen in a South Indian village.

It is a fact well known even to the most superficial observer of Hindu society that every portion of the system upon which that society has been constructed is tinged with religion. The Hindus are essentially a religious people, and our ancient lawgivers taking advantage of this characteristic of the nation, constructed a system which was made to be religiously binding. The manners, the customs, and the ordinary daily duties have their origin in religion. For instance, daily washing of the body, which is considered good from a sanitary point of view, is enjoined as a religious duty, and, even to this day, a person who disobeys this religious duty is shunned and avoided by his friends. Thus, in fact, the Hindu lives, moves, and has his being in religion.

Besides this, it is a fact also well known that there is no nation in the world so conservative as the Hindus—no people who stick with such wonderful tenacity to the manners and customs instituted by their forefathers as we ourselves. Ask a Hindu why he follows this custom or that, and he will immediately say that his father taught him to do so, and that it was handed down to him from time immemorial. And yet to none are the words of the poet—

> "We think our fathers fools, so wise we grow;
> No doubt our wiser sons will think us so,"

more applicable than to many of us of the present generation.

No doubt, the Mohammedan conquest, which was felt in a greater or less degree for nearly seven centuries, and the influence of Western civilization modified to a great extent our beliefs and superstitions. But the Mohammedan conquest was felt only in Northern India, where its influence has been most marked. Southern India was rarely visited by the followers of the Prophet; they simply pounced upon it occasionally for the sake of plunder. In proof of this, we note the fact that large temples and religious institutions founded by Hindu rajahs in the south remain intact. The cruel hand of the Mohammedan did not demolish those wonderful architectural structures that remain even to this day. We note also the fact that, while the languages of Northern India have been considerably affected by Mohammedan contact, the Dravidian languages of the south retain a special distinctiveness of their own. Again, the influence of Western civilization is felt only in large towns, and it has not yet penetrated into the inner recesses of Indian villages. It is, therefore, to the villages of Southern India that we must go to see Hindu life at its best, unaffected as it is either by the Mohammedan conquest or by the influence of Western civilization. Life in a South Indian village presents many interesting points to the historian and to the student of antiquities.

There are about 55,000 villages in the Madras Presidency, and out of a population of about thirty-one millions, nearly twenty-eight millions or about 90 per cent. of the whole population of the presidency live in villages, while the remaining 10 per cent. live in towns. In trying to describe the manner in which the bulk of the people inhabiting Southern India spend their lives in their village homes, I shall take a typical village and describe it by enumerating the different persons living in it and the several duties they perform.

A cluster of trees consisting of the tamarind, mango, cocoanut, plantain and other useful Indian trees, a group of dwellings, some thatched and some tiled, a small temple in the centre—these surrounded on all sides by about five hundred acres of green fields, and a large tank capable of watering those five hundred acres of land for about six months—this is the village of Kélambakam, situated in the Chingleput district, midway between Conjeeveram, and Mahabalipuram, two very old and important towns that played a most conspicuous part in the ancient history of Southern India. For over five hundred years, from the fifth century after Christ, the Pallavas, a powerful race of kings, carried on a constant warfare with the Chalukyans, and the country between these two ancient towns was the scene of many a pitched battle between the two races. Ancient inscriptions relate how the Pallavas were constantly harassed by their enemies, how, consequently, they held sway, at one time in Conjeeveram, at another in Mahabalipuram, and how badly the vanquished and their country were treated by the victorious. The result of this constant antagonism was that the country became almost a deserted waste in spite of its natural fertility. The soil is rich and the broad Palar runs through it. The hand of man was the only thing wanting to convert the arid plains into smiling green fields. Of course, we, who live under favourable conditions, may be disposed to think that the picture I have drawn exists only in imagination, but when we read that, for nearly six centuries, there was constant warfare, that the vanquished "were trodden to death by elephants in battle," and that all the rules of modern warfare were unknown in those days, we need not wonder that the country between Conjeeveram and Mahabalipuram was most devoid of cultivation and uninhabited. It was not till after the middle of the eleventh century that a deliverer appeared on the scene in the person of Adondai, son of Kulotunga Chola, who finally put an end to the conflict between the two contending races and established his own supremacy with Conjeeveram for his capital. It was not till after that time that peace was restored and the country settled down.

Kélambakam accordingly came into existence about the end of the eleventh century. It comprises some fifty or sixty houses, and has a population of about three hundred. The most influential people in the village are Tuluva Vellalas, and there are about ten families belonging to that caste living in it. Tradition says that Adondai, after he conquered the country, brought people from the Tuluva country to colonize his newly conquered dominions, and that he gave them lands to cultivate on easy terms. Even to this day we find Tuluva Vellalas, a very respectable class of people, scattered over the whole of Thondamandalam—the country conquered by Adondai. The headman of the village, or, as he is commonly called, the village munsiff, is Kothundarama Mudelly, a Tuluva Vellala by caste. He owns some fifty acres of land in the village. His father, a very pious man, left him the sole heir of all his properties. His ancestors were Saivites by religion, but the family, in common with others, embraced Vaishnavism about the 12th or the 13th century, when the great reformer Ramanuja went about the country preaching and converting people. It was about this time that the temple above-mentioned and dedicated to *Kothundarama* was built by one of the village munsiff's ancestors in his zeal for the religion which he had newly embraced, and the present Kothundarama Mudelly was named by his father after the idol. The villagers place the highest confidence in him. He is respected by the people of the village, not so much owing to the fact of his being the village munsiff as for his sterling worth. He is

> "beloved by all its men,
> Their friend in times of need, their guide in life,
> Partaker of their joys and woes as well,
> The arbiter of all their petty strifes."

As village munsiff, the whole management of the village is vested in him. He has the power of deciding petty civil cases, and also of trying persons for petty crimes. He can impose slight fines and give a few hours imprisonment. The imprisonment is not real, and the power of awarding it is scarcely exercised. In the case of Sudras, the accused person is put in charge of the *taliyari*, the village police peon, and in the case of Pariahs and other low caste people the accused person's hands or legs are shoved into a wooden instrument with large holes, and the criminal is made to remain in that humiliating posture for several hours. This is the kind of imprisonment the munsiff has the power of administering, but, as I said before, he very rarely exercises that power. The headman has also the power of collecting revenues from the ryots, of granting them receipts, and he remits the money to the taluk treasury. He must report to the head of the taluk (sub-division of a district) serious cases of theft and accidental deaths, send regularly a statement of the rainfall of the village, and of births and deaths, assist the authorities, revenue or other, in their official duties, and even supply those authorities with necessary provisions, when they go there in their official capacity or for the sake of pleasure. These with his own duties of looking after the cultivation of his fifty acres of land occupy a good deal of his time. Kélambakam, which is situated on the road between Conjeeveram and Tirukalukunram, where there is a very important Siva shrine, is a halting place for religious mendicants travelling to and fro. To these Kothundarama Mudelly every day distributes rice, and it is a pleasure to him to collect stray travellers halting for the night in his village and take supper with them. In the village, he has to do a thousand and one things. He has to settle disputes arising between the villagers, preside at festivals, marriages, and other social gatherings. In short, he is the most important man in the village, and well might he exclaim in the words of Alexander Selkirk—

> "I am the monarch of all I survey,
> My right there is none to dispute."

Next in importance to Munsiff Kothundarama Mudelly is Ramasami Pillai, the kurnam or the accountant of the village. He has to keep a register of accounts. He is expected to know the extent, name, rent, &c., of every field in the village; he has to assist the munsiff in preparing accounts, when money is remitted. Whenever the villagers have letters to write to relations, documents to be executed and calculations of interest to be made, when disputes arise, the assistance of the infallible kurnam is invoked, as he is considered to be the neatest writer and the most accurate accountant of the village. Ramasami Pillai is a mighty person in the village, and he is also a wily person. There is a Tamil proverb—"Confide if you will in the young one of a crow, but never believe the son of a kurnam." The kurnam, though he may be a good man, has come to be regarded with distrust by the villagers, and such is the case with Ramasami Pillai. Nobody would dare to oppose him or incur his displeasure. Nevertheless, the simple villagers go to him whenever they have any business transactions, for nobody else in the village can perform their work so well as he, and Ramasami Pillai calculated interest so quickly, wrote documents so neatly and accurately, and, readily gave out, without reference to his register, whatever information was wanted regarding each and every plot of land in the village, that the people of Kélambakam viewed him with admiration and wondered—

"That one small head could carry all he knew."

Next comes Muthu Naick, the taliyari, or the person who does the duties of the police in the village. He is a tall, powerful, broad-chested man, fair in complexion, of middle age, and carries a strong bamboo stick, some six feet in length. He has to assist the munsiff in cases civil and criminal, and when persons are convicted by the munsiff, Muthu Naick is the jailor. He has to watch the villages at nights, patrol the fields when crops are ripe and see that no thefts occur. He has also to go to the treasury in charge of money when remittances are sent from the village. Such are the duties discharged by the *village munsiff*, the *kurnam*, and the *taliyari*.

II.

The Hindu system of caste—The Puróhitā, or the astrologer—The temple priests—The schoolmaster.

A THOUGHTFUL Englishman, who, I know, has the true interests of India at heart, once observed to me that the greatest stumbling-block to the regeneration of India is *caste*. Opinions are divided amongst earnest thinkers with regard to this peculiar system which has for ages existed in this country. But whatever may be the opinions held either in favour of, or against, caste, it cannot be doubted for a moment that this great social system has played a most prominent part in the history of India and has had a strong hold upon the minds of the people. The four castes, namely, the Brahmin, the Kshathriya, the Vysia, and the Sudra, are said to have come from the head, arms, loins, and feet of Brahma, and each has for generations performed its allotted work. While the Kshathriya, with the strength of his arms, conquered new dominions and shed his blood in securing peace to the country from foreign aggression, while the Vysia toiled hard and amassed wealth by tending cattle, by tilling the soil and by trading, and while the Sudra performed menial service, the Brahmin always carried the palm for intellectual greatness and held the others under his magic influence. By the strength of his intellect he has moulded the thoughts and guided the feelings of the people to such an extent that a foreign observer may well stand amazed at the result.

> "He waved the sceptre o'er his kind,
> By nature's first great title mind."

So in Kélambakam, the Brahmin Ramanuja Charriar, the Purohita, is the friend, guide, and philosopher of the village. His influence over the villagers is very great. He is a venerable old gentleman of three score and ten years, well versed in the Hindu Shastras. He knows a little of Sanskrit and has read many books on astrology. He could repeat by heart all the four thousand stanzas of the sacred *Prabhan-*

tham, usually called the Tamil Vedas. He is considered by every villager as part and parcel of his family, and the simple villager dare not do anything without consulting him.

Ramanuja Charriar owns a house near the temple of the village. It has a decent appearance. On the floor near the entrance are quaint figures drawn with rice powder, and on the wall facing the street are to be seen representations of the coronation of Rama, of Krishna tending cattle and playing on the flute, of Narasimha killing the giant king, and many other figures which at once convince the stranger that the occupant of the house must be a person steeped in religion.

The old gentleman rises very early in the morning, bathes in the tank, puts on the usual marks on his forehead and other parts of his body, performs the Pujah and returns home.

He then sets out with a cadjan (palmyra leaf) book, which is the calendar for the year, and first goes to the house of the village munsiff Kothundarama Mudelly. The munsiff, as soon as he sees the Brahmin, rises and salutes him, and asks him to take a seat. The Purohita opens his book and reads from it in a loud voice the particulars of the day—the year, the month, and the date, the portions that are auspicious and those that are not, &c. While this recital goes on, the munsiff is all attention. Soon after, an old woman, the mother of Kothundarama Mudelly, steps in and asks the astrologer on what day the new moon falls, and when the anniversary of the death of her husband should be celebrated. The munsiff perhaps asks him if, according to his horoscope, the year will on the whole be a prosperous one for him and if his lands will bring forth abundance of grain. To such questions, the Purohita answers according to the rules of astrology. He goes in like manner to the house of every villager, and various are the questions put to him. One villager asks him to appoint an auspicious day for buying bullocks to plough his fields; another asks him to name a propitious hour for commencing the building of a house; a third asks him to select a day for the marriage of his aged daughter and shows him the horoscope of his would-be son-in-law; a fourth asks him to fix a day on which to go to the neighbouring village to bring his daughter-in-law home; a fifth asks him when such and such a feast comes ; a sixth puts into his hands the horoscope of his sick son and asks him if he will recover ; a seventh requests him to prepare the horoscope of his newly-born child and furnishes him with the exact time when the child first saw the light of day ; the next person complains to him about the loss of a jewel, and asks him to name the person who stole it, to describe the place where it is hidden, and so on. To all these questions, the Purohita, opening his book, gives suitable answers, and, to illustrate his statements, he even quotes Sanskrit slokas, stanzas from the *Ramayana*, the *Mahabharatha* and the sacred *Prabhantham*, and verses from works on astrology. These quotations create very strong impressions, "for, in the East," as Sir Walter Scott says, "wisdom is held to consist, less in a display of the sage's own inventive talents, than in his ready memory, and happy application of, and reference to, 'that which is written.'" Any instructions given by him are obeyed to the very letter. The ryots will not begin to cultivate, to sow their lands, or to reap their harvest without first consulting him as to the auspicious time. The Brahmin also officiates as priest on marriage and funeral occasions, and is the principal actor during feasts, which are of almost daily occurrence in a Hindu family. There is a Tamil proverb which says that "The Vydian or the doctor will not leave the patient till he dies, but that the Brahmin will not leave him even after his death." Even during the last moments of the patient the doctor says that if he is given a handsome fee, he will effect an immediate cure by administering a valuable medicine which is in his possession, and which was prepared by his great-grandfather after a great deal of labour and expense. He thus imposes upon the credulity of the people till death snatches the patient from them: the Brahmin's connection does not cease with the death of the patient. He must perform the first day's ceremonies, as also those of the second, eighth, and sixteenth days. Then come the monthly and yearly ceremonies, at which the Brahmin plays an important part.

Such is a brief description of the old sage of Kélambakam, whose influence even in the neighbouring villages is very great, and whom the villagers regard with feelings of deep veneration.

There are, besides the house of the Purohita, two other houses near the temple belonging to Brahmins who do work in the temple. In one lives Varadayyangar and in the other his brother Appalacharri. They perform the Pujah of the temple by turns, and lead a very easy life. Persons who go to the temple to worship the idol take with them offerings in the shape of money, fruit, coconúts, betel and nut, &c. These are appropriated by the brothers. There are about seven acres of land in the village set apart for the temple, and the income derived therefrom goes towards the expenses incurred for the lighting of the temple, the daily rice offerings, and the salaries of the servants; and, as the brothers are the principal servants of the temple, they come in for a good share of the income. Besides these, they get extra income on festival occasions, when the idol is decked with jewels and flowers and carried in procession. Appalacharri is of a quarrelsome disposition, and numerous have been the disputes between the brothers with regard to the temple income. Kothundarama Mudelly, the Dhurmakurta, has often a good deal of difficulty in settling their differences; and he it was who decided that they should do their work by turns, and that each should receive the income derived during his term of office. Appalacharri, not content with quarrelling with his own brother, has often employed his spare time in fomenting quarrels among the villagers, and were it not for the tact and good sense of the village munsiff and the quiet nature of the people of the village, Kélambakam would be a different place from what it now is. Such a mischievous disposition is that of Appalacharri that a complete enumeration of his doings would occupy a whole paper.

There are at the present moment scattered throughout the length and breadth of Southern India thousands of educated natives performing honourable work with distinction both to themselves and to their country. Most of these sat at the feet of such distinguished educationists as Dr. Miller and Messrs. Porter, Powell, and Thompson, and their veneration for their former masters is as deep and sincere as that held for the great master of Rugby by his students. And if it is asked, why it is that, in this country, *hero-worship* in the case of the schoolmaster is carried to such an extent, I would reply that it is a characteristic of the Hindu to honour and respect his intellectual guide. In India, the pial schoolmasters are an honourable body of men who do their work in an unassuming manner and enjoy the esteem and good will of the people.

Nalla Pillai is the schoolmaster of Kélambakam, and he is next in importance to the Purohita. He is a great-great-grandson of Nalla Pillai, the reputed author of the *Mahabharatha* in Tamil verse. Our village schoolmaster was named after him, and he knows by heart all the fourteen thousand stanzas of the book. He preserves with pride and pleasure the style with which his illustrious ancestor wrote his great work, and the style is worshipped in his house every year on the Ayuthapuja day. Nalla Pillai's school is located in the pial of his house. The attendance is between twenty and thirty, and even boys from the neighbouring villages come here to be instructed. The boys are seated in two rows on a raised basement in the outer part of the house, and the master is seated at one end of the pial. There is a radical difference between the system of instruction imparted in English schools and that in vogue in these village seats of learning. In the former a great deal of time and labour is saved by having a number of boys conveniently arranged into classes so that they may be all taught at the same time. In the latter the teacher goes through the lessons with each boy separately. In the school of the village before us, three or four youngsters, between five and seven years of age, are seated in a row learning the letters of the alphabet by uttering them aloud and writing them on sand strewn on the floor. One or two are writing the letters on cadjan leaves. One boy is reading in a loud voice words from a cadjan book, while another reads short sentences. A third is working sums in arithmetic. A fourth is reciting poetical stanzas in a drawling tone, and a fifth is reading verses from Nalla Pillai's *Mahabharatha* before the master, who, after the reading is over, explains their meaning to the boy. A boy is said to have completed his education if he is able to read and write accurately anything on a cadjan leaf and know the simple and compound rules of arithmetic and simple interest, and such proficiency may be attained after four or five years' study in the village school.

The boys go to school before six in the morning, return home for breakfast at nine, go back to school at ten, and remain there till two, when they are allowed to go for their midday meal. They then return to school at three, and remain there till it gets dark. Thus it will be seen that the schoolmaster is at work from early morn till eve, going through the lessons of each individual boy. The school is closed for four days in the month, namely on the day of new moon and the day after, and on the day of full moon and the day after. The boys are also allowed leave on festival days.

The teacher, besides the remuneration paid to him by the parents, not infrequently gets extra income in the shape of money, new clothes, vegetables, &c., when boys are newly sent to school and when marriages and festivals take place. The schoolmaster is expected to look after the children of the villagers and to take an interest in their welfare not only in the school but in their homes. If it is reported that a boy is ill and that he refuses to take medicine, the master is expected to go to his house and see that the medicine is administered. If a boy has an aversion to taking meals, or if he becomes mischievous and troublesome out of school hours, his parents at once invoke the assistance of the teacher, who must go to the house of the erring youth and see that such things do not recur. The village master is thus constantly sought after by the villagers, and he is their most useful friend.

I must not fail to notice that the village teacher makes it a special part of his duty to give religious instruction. The work of the school commences and closes every day with a prayer to *Saraswati*, the goddess of learning, or *Vigneswara*, a Hindu deity supposed to preside over the destinies of men. All the boys are expected to get these prayers by heart and repeat them aloud. The youths are also made to get by heart during holidays some poetical stanzas containing moral maxims on cadjan leaves, at the top of which there always appears some religious symbol or saying such as the following :—*Victory be to Rama ; Siva is everywhere.* The boys are always taught to fear God, to be honest and truthful, to venerate their parents and superiors, and so on. It will thus be seen that religious teaching forms a part and a very important part in the work of a village schoolmaster.

Regarding the punishment inflicted on the boys, I must say that Nalla Pillai is an honourable exception to those teachers who often have recourse to the most barbarous modes of chastising youths. I shall therefore not detain my readers with an explanation of those modes of punishment.

Besides the work that Nalla Pillai has in the school, he is often engaged in the evening reciting verses from the *Mahabharatha* and explaining their meaning to the villagers.

> "And oft at night when ended was their toil,
> The villagers with souls enraptured heard him
> In fiery accents speak of Krishna's deeds
> And Rama's warlike skill, and wondered that
> He knew so well the deities they adored."

From the above short description of the village schoolmaster we see that he is a very important element in the village constitution. He is honoured and respected by the people, and regarded by them as a friend and counsellor. Recourse is constantly had to his assistance in reading and writing letters and in the settling of disputes. He is freely admitted to their homes and invited on festival days. Nalla

Pillai does his work, day after day, month after month, year after year, in an unostentatious and quiet way, enjoying the esteem and good will of all the villagers and the love of his pupils.

III.

Hindu poetry—The physician—The carpenter—The blacksmith—The shepherd—The story of the dull shepherd.

IN speaking of Indian poetry, Dr. Miller, in his introduction to my "Tales of Ind," very justly observed :—"Whatever else she may have wanted, India has never wanted poetry. In some form, whether good or bad, whether high or low, the poetic instincts of her children have found expression in every succeeding age of her chequered history." Her gifted sons wrote poems that are read with delight and admiration by the modern world. They wrote poetry, true poetry, which purifies and ennobles man, which "offers interesting objects of contemplation to the sensibilities," and "delineates the deeper and more secret workings of human emotion." But at the same time, our countrymen wrote poetry, which is nothing more than mere *metrical com-*

position, and it must be said that in India, more than in any other country, poetry has degenerated so much that it has been used as a vehicle for conveying information in almost every conceivable subject. Our astronomy, our astrology, and our works on medicine are written in poetry, and only the other day I was startled to hear an expert in valuing precious stones quote stanza after stanza from an ancient Tamil work describing the quality and colour of rubies. The colour of a certain kind of rubies the author compares to that of the blood of the sparrow just killed. Another kind there is whose colour is like that of the setting sun, and so on. All this could very well be described in prose, but the author has foolishly spent a great deal of time and labour in versifying what he wanted to say. No doubt this mode of conveying information has its advantages. In an age when printing was unknown, when books were written on cadjan leaves, it could not be expected that people would possess a sufficient number of books to read. Many valuable Hindu works have been handed down to posterity in the same manner as the Greek Rhapsodists are said to have handed down the poetry of Homer. They were committed to memory and transmitted to succeeding generations—a process very much facilitated by the fact that they were expressed in poetry.

I have been led to indulge in these general remarks, because Appasami Vathiar, who is the *vythian* or physician of Kèlambakam and who is the next person claiming our attention, always quoted from *Vagadam*, a Tamil work on medicine written in verse. In describing a disease he quoted from *Vagadam*. In prescribing medicines, he quoted from *Vagadam*, and even in giving instructions to people in the matter of diet, the same favourite *Vagadam* was called into requisition. The Hindu's reverence for anything old and mystical is very great, and Appasami Vathiar was held in great esteem by the people of Kélambakam and the surrounding villages, because, in his practice, he did not swerve one jot or tittle from what has been laid down in Hindu works on medicine. It is a prevalent belief among Hindus—and Appasami Vathiar did much in his own way to strengthen that belief—that our forefathers attained perfection in medicine, and that it is not capable of further improvement.

The general complaint is that the vythians now-a-days do not read old Hindu books on medicine, and practise it according to the directions given in them.

Our village doctor knows nothing of surgery. He is a physician, pure and simple. He is a *Virasiva* by religion, and is said to have read a good many medical books. He is about fifty years of age, and enjoys a very good practice. He knows a little of astrology, but does not claim to know so much of it as Ramanuja Charriar, the Purohita. Like the Purohita and the schoolmaster, he is honoured and respected by the people of Kélambakam, and they have implicit confidence in his skill and ability. He carries with him all kinds of medicines in the shape of pills and powders. He is said to know the nature of a man's complaint by feeling his pulse. He does not believe in the efficacy of medicine alone, but always takes care to impress upon the relatives of his patients the necessity of performing some religious ceremony or other to appease the anger of the gods. The simple villagers have so much faith in him that even if death takes away the patient, they attribute it not to any want of skill on his part, but to the stars that guided the patient's destinies having been unfavourable. Once Appasami Vathiar was absent from the village for a number of days, and Kothundarama Mudelly, the village munsiff, was at the time attacked with fever. It gradually grew worse, and the village munsiff's relatives began to entertain grave doubts about his recovery. News of this was sent to the vythian, who returned in haste to attend the patient. It was early in the morning when he entered the house of the village munsiff, and there in the *Kutam* or hall he saw the patient leaning upon his old mother and surrounded by a number of sorrowing relatives and friends. The Purohita was seated in one part of the hall with some villagers looking at the sick man's horoscope, making calculations and finding whether the malady would prove fatal. But the scene was changed the moment the vythian entered the house and sat by the sick man. The face of the old mother, down whose wrinkled cheeks tears were flowing in abundance, now beamed with joy, and the relatives who a minute ago were filled with despair were now animated with hope. They whispered to one another that Kothundarama Mudelly's recovery was beyond all doubt. So sudden and complete was the transformation. The vythian then felt the pulse of the sick man and quoted some verses from the *Vagadam* describing the malady, to which the mother nodded her head and said that the symptoms of the disease therein enumerated were noticed in her sick son. Then said the vythian: "The malady has assumed serious proportions. *Yama* is fast overtaking the sick person. Here is the medicine *Mrityunjayam* (conqueror of death) which will put a stop to his deadly course. This medicine which my great grandfather prepared with the assistance of a rich zemindar must be continued for three days, and after that time the patient must take another medicine *Jivarakshamritham* (the ambrosia that saves life), which I prepared last year after consulting many shastras, spending about five cartloads of fuel, fasting for forty days, and feeding one hundred mendicants. The patient will gradually recover. But at the same time I must ask you to light ten lamps in the temple every day and feed six Brahmins till such time as the patient recovers." So saying he took from his medicine pouch two pills, mixed them in honey, and administered the same to the patient. Then after giving instructions with regard to diet, &c., patiently answering the thousand and one anxious questions put to him by the relatives of the patient, and restoring confidence in them, and after promising to return in the evening, he departed. In ten days' time the patient recovered, and this incident raised the vythian all the more in the estimation of the people of Kélambakam. Such is a short account of the village doctor, Appasami Vathiar, in whose skill the simple people of the village had the greatest confidence and for whose integrity and high character they had the highest respect.

Next comes the carpenter Soobroya Acharry. His business is to make ploughs (Indian ploughs are made of wood with an iron bar fixed to the end) and all sorts of wooden implements required for the purpose of cultivation. He has to make carts and boxes and assist the villagers in the construction of houses. The village carpenter's work is not such as would excite the admiration of the beholder or be considered worthy of being shown at an exhibition. It is a plain, rough kind of work just good enough to answer the purpose intended. Soobroya Acharry has also to make for the villagers pestles and a number of wooden instruments required for daily use.

After Soobroya Acharry comes Shunmugam, the blacksmith of the village, who is required to do his portion of the work in the construction of houses and in the making of agricultural and other implements. He has to make axes for hewing down trees, sickles with which to reap corn, spades, crowbars, and a number of other useful and necessary things. From the above it will be seen that the carpenter and the blacksmith are very useful members of the community, and that their services are often called into requisition by the villagers.

Another very important and useful member of the community is Gopaula Pillai, the *ideiyan* or shepherd. He owns a number of cows and buffaloes and supplies the villages with ghee (clarified butter), milk and curds ; he also looks after their cattle. He is a very busy man. He rises early in the morning and goes to the houses of the villagers to milk their cows, and returns at about nine o'clock. In the meantime, his wife Seeta, who is a good model of a busy helpmate, is engaged in cleansing the cattle-shed, milking her own cows and buffaloes, churning butter and selling milk and curds. As soon as the cowherd comes home, he takes his *canji* (boiled rice and water). He then goes away with the cattle of the village to the grazing fields. There are some fine pasture lands at a distance of about two miles from Kélambakam where the cowherds and shepherds of other villages meet our ideiyan friend, Gopaula Pillai. There, while the cattle graze, these simple men beguile their time under the shade of some tree in innocent talk or in some game. The cowherd returns with the cattle to the village at dusk and goes again to the houses of such villagers as have cows, to milk them. He returns home at about eight at night, and after taking supper enjoys a well-earned sleep. It is said that shepherds are dull and stupid, and there are many stories current among the people illustrative of this fact. Here is a story which is often told :—

THE IDEIYAN.[1]

'Mong Hindu Castes, the Ideiyars are dull;
Brains wanting, Nature gives them but a skull;

[1] From the *Madras Mail.*

Hence as the Tamil proverb truly tells,
In nape of neck all ideiyan wisdom dwells.

One of this Jathi, who was far from wise,
Even in his lotus-faced pendatti's (wife's) eyes,
Resisted bravely with ideiyan might,
The entrance of one ray of wisdom's light.

She tried all arts as Hindu women can
On this unyielding matter—called a man.
She coaxed him, boxed him, scolded him and squeezed;
Unchanged, he only ate, and slept, and sneezed.

Anon with honied words as poets sing,
She spoke :—he was her guru, god and king.
Her neighbours smiled :—" when horses horned you see,
Your silent, senseless guru wise may be."

To cheer the villagers one day there came
The singer Thumbiran well known to fame;
Of Rama, Seeta, Ravana, he sang,
And through bazaar and street his music rang.

Men left their homes and work, and came from far,
And hailed him as another Avatar :—
" Ramayanam will make my husband wise,
Perchance, and end my contless toils and sighs."

So thought this good pendatti, strongly bent
On making wise her ideiyan lord, and sent
Him forth to hear the singer. He obeyed,—
As Ideiyars should, and listened undismayed.

In ideiyan posture, on his staff his chin
He rested, as to drink the nectar in.
A waggish neighbour saw his vacant stare,
Leapt on his back, and calmly listened there.

Part of the programe this,—the ideiyan deemed;
A waggish trick his burden never seemed.
Thus seeking wisdom, stood he in the sun
Well weighted, listening till the song was done.

Then homeward, weary grown, if still not wise;
Homeward to meet his lovely Seeta's eyes,
The hero went. She, through the window bars,
Peeped, waiting for his coming,—as the stars.

Hoping to see her ideiyan's face divine,
With light of new found wisdom brightly shine;
"What say you of Ramayanam?" she began;
He answered;—"Tis as heavy as a man."

She whispered to the sky at this response;
"He born an ideiyan must die a dunce;—
"Fate wills it, unreversed, while ages roll
"If Kamban cannot stir his boorish soul."

The above is one of the many stories current about the dulness and stupidity of the shepherd. Nevertheless, he is honest, straightforward, and guileless. His wants are few and his cattle are his only care. His lot in life has many a time warned man not to pant after vain glory. It has been the favourite theme of poets in all ages and in all climes, and the envy of philosophers.

IV.

The washerman—The potter—The barber and his wife, the village midwife—The Pujari, or the priest of the village goddess.

It is said that the village washerman has scarcely leisure to attend to his own domestic duties. This is no doubt true, for Munian, the washerman of Kélambakam, is the most hard-working member of the village. He rises early every morning and, with an earthen vessel, goes to the village in one direction, while his wife goes in another, to collect dirty clothes. On reaching the house of a villager, he informs the people of his arrival by making a noise which at once brings out a female, who hands over to him such clothes as require washing, with perhaps some special instructions in the case of particular clothes, and then supplies him with a handful of the Indian preparation called *kulu*—raggi flour cooked with broken rice—

which he deposits in the earthen vessel. He returns home at about nine or ten o'clock. His wife returns at about the same time with a potful of *kulu* and a bundle of clothes. They then with their children partake of what they have collected from the villagers, and go to the river Palar with the dirty clothes to wash them. There, with scarcely any intermission, they toil hard in the heat of the sun, and by dusk they have washed the clothes that were entrusted to them in the morning. They then return to the village and arrange the clothes of each household with a precision which is most astonishing, and which most probably gave rise to the saying that a washerman is more useful than an educated person. After this, they set out to the village to deliver the clothes. This time, instead of a pot, they carry each a basket in which to carry the cooked rice supplied to them by the villagers. They return home at about nine or ten, take their supper and go to sleep, which they have richly earned after a hard day's toil. Even this little rest is denied to the poor washerman whenever festivals are celebrated in the temple or when dramatic performances are given in the village, as on those occasions he is expected to prepare torches with torn clothes collected by himself, and look after the lights. Thus, Munian, the washerman of Kélambakam, with Lakshmi, his exemplary wife and useful assistant, willingly performs, without the least murmur, the arduous task allotted to him in his little village world.

Another member of the village, as useful and almost as hardworking as the washerman, is Kuppusami, the potter, who toils at his wheel day and night to supply the villagers with earthen vessels. He has to make earthen lamps, cooking vessels, huge jars for storing grain, bricks, tiles, &c., for building houses, drinking vessels and a hundred other things required for an Indian household. He has also to make figures of human shape, and such like things for use in the temple of the village deity. Any stranger going into the house of a Hindu will at once be struck with the usefulness of the potter, when he finds whole rooms containing earthen vessels of different sizes and shapes arranged like conically shaped pillars, each containing some article of human consumption. On important festival occasions, such as the Pungul, Kuppusami has to supply every house in Kélambakam with new vessels, and, on occasions of marriage, he has to prepare big pots ornamented with quaint figures. His assistance is also sought after in accidents when bones are broken or fractured. I do not know how the potter has come to be regarded as the fittest person to treat such cases. Man, it is said, is made of clay by Brahma, who is often compared to a potter. And the potter, who makes figures of human form is expected to know the constitution of the human frame. Hence probably arose the idea that he is the fittest person to treat cases of fracture, &c. Kuppusami is skilful in the treatment of such cases, and his practice extends even to the neighbouring villages.

After the potter, comes Kailasam, the *ambattan*, the barber of the village. He also is a very useful member of Kélambakam. He is the village hair-dresser. He is also the musician of his village. Without music, no festival can be celebrated in the temple, no marriage or any other ceremony can take place in an Indian household ; and on those occasions Kailasam and his people are required to play on the flute, beat drums, &c. Kailasam is also the surgeon of Kélambakam, and it is somewhat difficult to account for the fact that barbers have been allowed to practise surgery. They are considered to be the fittest persons to treat surgical cases, probably because, as barbers, they handle the knife. Thoyamma, the wife of Kailasam, is the midwife of the village. Her attendance is also required every day, morning and evening, to look after newly-born infants, to bathe them, to administer to them proper medicines and do many other things which need not be enumerated here.

Every village in Southern India has a temple built in honour of a goddess, who, it is said, guards the village from all kinds of pestilential diseases, such as smallpox, cholera, &c. The name of the goddess of Kélambakam is Angalammal, and the temple dedicated to her is situated a few furlongs from the village. Some lands in the village are allotted for the due performance of puja in the temple, and Angamuthu Pujaree, who performs the necessary ceremonies, enjoys those lands. When the country is afflicted with some pestilence, the pujaree levies all sorts of contributions from the simple villagers. To save them from infectious diseases, they present the deity with gold and silver ornaments, cloths, rice and vegetables, intoxicating liquors, sheep and fowls. These the pujaree appropriates to his own use. Worship in the temple of the village goddess is of a very low kind. Animals are sacrificed, intoxicating drugs are taken and crude songs are sung. Hideous dances also form part of the worship. Angamuthu Pujaree is a very intelligent man, and practises his trade with consummate skill. People from distant parts go to him on Thursdays, when, it is said, the spirit of the goddess Angalammal descends upon him and with such help he foretells events. With the pujaree the best art is to conceal art itself, and the more he fulfils this condition the more he succeeds and becomes popular. He has to be possessed of a certain amount of intelligence and tact if he is to perform his work aright. He has to weigh well all the circumstances of a case, and then decide what are suitable answers to give. Angamuthu Pujaree often gives, like the oracle of Delphi, dubious answers to questions put to him.

I was myself present with some of my friends at one of these meetings in the temple of the village goddess. There were then present people from distant villages. There were mothers with sick children. Near relatives of persons supposed to be the victims of sorcerers were there, anxiously waiting to get the blessing of the goddess through her favoured servant, the pujaree. There were collected in that motley assembly barren women anxious to get children, young bachelors eagerly waiting to know when they would get fair wives, and persons attacked with various kinds of disorders. There were about three hundred persons present on the occasion, some of whom came from places ten or twelve miles distant from Kélambakam. The goddess was neatly clothed and adorned with flowers. There was a black cane near the deity, which was afterwards used by the pujaree for driving out devils. Fruits and flowers and other presents there were in abundance, and there were also one or two bottles of intoxicating liquors, camphor and other things. The pujaree, after bathing and besmearing his body with ash, came and sat before Angalammal, to the immense delight of the expectant crowd. His assistants, with jingling instruments, sang some curious songs extolling the virtues of the goddess. The pujaree was all the while sitting in deep meditation. Then suddenly he swooned and fell down. Shortly after, he rose, took some liquor, and with a vigour and energy that would have done credit to the strongest acrobat, danced and jumped and made a most hideous and disgusting noise. Camphor was soon lighted. He took a long sword and inflicted all sorts of wounds on his body. The spirit of the goddess, it was said, had now fairly descended on him, and the terror-stricken people all gazed upon him with contending hopes and fears, to catch eagerly whatever was vouchsafed to them by their goddess through her servant. Then in deep clear tones, Angamuthu Pujaree uttered the following words: "A person of the male sex has come here to question me regarding a female relative. Let him come forward." There was deep silence and no one ventured to come forward. Again the pujaree said in a threatening tone: "I know the person. He is come here. Let him step forward without the least delay and kneel before me. If he does not, I will punish him." Immediately, a middle-aged person knelt before the pujaree and said: "Have mercy upon me O mother, I have come here to ask you if my sick wife will recover." The pujaree answered: "Your wife would have recovered long ago; but you have incurred my displeasure and to appease my anger you must sacrifice a sheep, and then your wife will recover." So saying the pujaree gave some ash to the supplicant to be smeared over his wife's body. Then said the pujaree: "A barren woman is here to ask me to bless her with a child. Where is she?" In due course, a young woman came forward, and to her he said: "You must for the next forty days bathe early in the morning and go round my temple nine times daily. You must take only one meal a day. And at the end of these forty days you must present me with a new cloth. You shall then be blessed with a child." After receiving some ash, the young woman retired. Then again the pujaree said: "A mother is come here with a sick child; let me see her." Immediately a sorrow-stricken woman placed a sick child before him. He threw some ash on the child and said: "Your child will recover in a fortnight, but do not fail to offer me a fowl."

"Yes, mother, I will do so," said the woman, and retired. In this way the pujaree put general questions, and people with various requests came forward. Suitable replies were vouchsafed to them, but the pujaree in every instance took care to ask various kinds of offerings. In the end, two things startled me, and I for a time at least thought the pujaree a veritable seer. The pujaree said: "A young man is come here to test me with a lemon concealed about him. He wishes to know when he will get married. Let him stand before me." Out stepped the young man, and, trembling with fear, delivered the lemon which he had kept concealed. Then again, the favoured servant of the goddess said: "An old man came to me last Thursday and said that, owing to the doings of a sorcerer, his son was suffering from various kinds of disorders." When the old man came forward, he continued: "Your enemy with the help of a sorcerer hid last month at midnight an earthen vessel in which are deposited human bones. So long as that vessel remains where it is, your son will not recover. Go now, with a dozen people from the assembly, and take out the vessel which is buried in the north-eastern corner of the cattle-shed of your house, some four feet and a half from the wall. Take it out and bring it to me." Immediately a number of people left the assembly and the pujaree went on attending to those who remained. Those who went, found in the exact spot described by the pujaree a vessel answering to his description, which they unearthed and brought to him, to the great amazement of the people assembled. The pujaree took it, and addressing the old man, said: "Go now. Your son will from this moment be all right." So saying he uttered an unintelligible *mantram* and dashed the vessel to the ground.

With regard to the first of the above incidents, I came to know a few days afterwards that the young man who came with the lemon unwittingly confided his secret to Appalacharri, one of the pujaree's secret agents, who freely mingled with the people as spectators. Appalacharri went and gave the information to the pujaree beforehand. The only possible explanation of the second is that the pujaree's assistants must themselves have buried the vessel with its contents.

The pujaree, it will thus be seen, is a most deceitful person practising his trade with success among the ignorant villagers. Happily under the benign British rule education is spreading fast, and the intelligence of the country is advancing at a rapid rate, and the day is not far distant when the wretched class of men, one of whom I have in the above pages tried to depict, will soon have vanished off the face of the land.

V.

The Panisiva—Account of the dispute between the Panisiva and the potter, and the part played therein by the Brahmin Appalacharri—The Shylock of Kélambakam—The dancing girls—The story of the shepherd and his wife.

When in olden days rules were framed for the proper management of Indian village constitutions, and particular duties were assigned to particular individuals, there were no easy means of communication in the country. It was therefore found necessary to have a separate class of men—the *Panisivas*—to carry to friends and relatives invitations to weddings, funerals, and special festival occasions, which, as I said in one of my previous papers, are of almost daily occurrence in Hindu families. The word *Panisiva* means literally one who serves; and Kanthan, the *Panisiva* of Kélambakam, is a hardworking, faithful, and willing servant of the villagers. He is required to blow the conch-shell during funerals, to serve betel and nut during marriages and festivals, to go even to distant villages to invite friends and relations to take part in those celebrations, and to do whatever other work is allotted to him on those occasions. By hard work and by the goodwill of the people of the village, he managed till very recently to live a happy life and even to save some money, The Brahmin Appalacharri very cleverly brought about an unnecessary quarrel between Kanthan, the *Panisiva*, and Kuppusami, the potter, they being neighbours, and by his scheming kept up the quarrel for some time. The result was that both of them figured many a time in the law courts, and learnt some very wholesome lessons after the expenditure of a good deal of money.

This is how the dispute arose. One day when Appalacharri was sorely in need of money, he went to the potter, who was toiling at his wheel, and very cleverly drew him into a conversation, in the course of which he said: "You know, Kuppusami, that there are two palmyra trees standing in the hedge, which separates your backyard from that of Kanthan. He enjoys their tender nuts and fruits. I do not see why you should not enjoy them also. Those trees stand in a common hedge, and in fact it is my strong conviction that they belong exclusively to you, and that the *Panisiva* has no right whatever to them." To this the potter said: "Yes, Swami! I also am entitled to enjoy the produce of the trees. I am sure to succeed if I can secure the assistance of one like you." "Do not be afraid," said the Brahmin, "the trees and the hedge will be yours." He then ask the potter to assist him with some money, which was willingly given.

The next day, Appalacharri sent for the *Panisiva*, and with the skill and tact so peculiar to him spoke about the hedge and the palmyra trees. "I know," he said, "the village headman Kothundarama Mudelly knows, and every one in the village also knows, that your father planted the two palmyra trees in your backyard, and who is there but you entitled to enjoy them? But the potter complained to me yesterday that you unjustly enjoy the tender nuts and the fruits. He says that he is entitled to a portion, if not the whole of the produce. I know that his demand is very unjust. But let me, as one that takes a deep interest in your welfare, tell you in all sincerity that he means some mischief; and before he does anything of that sort, see that you at once enclose the trees with prickly pear. If after that he tries to annoy you, come and tell me without a moment's delay." The *Panisiva* answered: Great Swami! I have no one else but you to assist me. I implore you on my feet to save me from the misdoings of my neighbour Kuppusami." "You can count upon my assistance," said the Brahmin. He then took some money from the poor *Panisiva* and sent him away with all sorts of assurances.

On the third day, the potter came running to Appalacharri and said: "My great Guru; you assured me the day before yesterday that I am the sole owner of the trees in the backyard, and that I alone am entitled to their produce. But last evening Kanthan fenced them round with prickly pear. You promised to use all your influence to secure for me the ownership of the trees as also the hedge. Here, my saviour, is some money for your gracious acceptance; please advise me what further I am to do." The Brahmin took the money, and advised him to go at once and pull down the fence. This was done, and immediately the *Panisiva* ran to Appalacharri with some money and told him that the potter had pulled down the fence; he then fell at Appalacharri's feet, cried like a child, and begged of him to do all that could be done. To this the Brahmin angrily said: "You are a fool; you cry like a child. You should have manfully kicked the potter, when he removed the fencing. Here I will write a complaint for you; go and lodge it at once before the magistrate." The complaint was thrown out, as the dispute was said to be of a civil nature. The *Panisiva* then filed a civil suit. During the progress of the suit the court had to appoint a commissioner to inspect the spot and submit a report, and during all this time Appalacharri exacted as much money as possible from both. In the end, after the lapse of two years of anxious care and toil and after the expenditure of a large sum of money, the *Panisiva's* just title to the trees was recognized by the court, and the foolish potter, who was unwillingly dragged into the quarrel, learnt a dearly bought lesson. Thus were two simple villagers nearly ruined by unnecessary litigation cleverly brought about by the wily machinations of an uncrupulous Brahmin.

The person next claiming our attention is Muthusami Chetty, the Shylock of Kélambakam, and he is not one whit better than the leech-like village usurer, about whom one hears so much nowadays. This man, who belongs to the trading class, lives in a strong, well-built house to which is attached a spacious granary. He owns the only bazaar in Kélambakam, and it is located in the pial of his house. He makes periodical visits to the nearest town, and buys whatever articles of consumption are required for his village. These he sells either for money or for grain. The system of paying revenue to Government in money and by monthly instalments, from December to May, is very favourable to the money-lending classes of the community, and it has been and still is the means of easily enriching them and making them more prosperous than the rest of the people. The villager who is in need of say a hundred rupees for paying Government revenue, has simply to go to our Chetty friend, who gives the required amount, on the condition that it is repaid in grain at the harvesting season.

No interest is charged by the money-lender. Now the average price of paddy during the harvesting season, which commences in January and extends till March, is 27 measures for a rupee. Thus the villager, who borrowed one hundred rupees, has to give the money-lender 2,700 measures of paddy. This the latter stores in his granary, and sells in July, August, and September, when the average market price is 19 measures for a rupee; so that Muthusami Chetty's one hundred rupees amount to nearly one hundred and fifty rupees in about six months. This arrangement tells very heavily upon the cultivating classes, but they cannot help it. Again, whenever they have to buy bullocks for ploughing, when they have to build houses, to marry their sons or daughters, or to perform funeral ceremonies in honour of departed relatives (and marriages and funeral ceremonies are very expensive in Hindu families), they must go to the village usurer and borrow money on the same rigid conditions. Here, indeed, is a splendid opportunity for Hindu capitalists. Instead of devising all sorts of means for investing their capital, they should start agricultural banks and lend money to the cultivating classes. By so doing they would not only get fair interest for their money, but would be the means of saving thousands of families from ruin, of making them more prosperous and happy, and of effacing a class of people who live upon the labour of others, and are draining the life-blood of the agricultural population of the land.

Our village usurer Muthusami Chetty is a cunning and clever man of business. He looks after his bazaar, keeps the accounts regularly, and does all the business himself without the assistance of a clerk. He is also a very safe man, and does not give offence to people even when they give him cause to do so. He aims at pleasing each and every one in the village, and the following story which I heard of him illustrates very well this characteristic. One day, two persons, who went to make purchases from his bazaar, unfortunately quarrelled. Hot words were exchanged, and, notwithstanding Muthusami's remonstrances, words came to blows. In the end, both complained to the magistrate, and both cited the Chetty as their witness. He, to please both, addressed the magistrate thus: "Maharajah! I have been unnecessarily dragged here to give evidence. One day these two persons now standing before your august presence, came to my bazaar to buy certain articles. They quarrelled and each abused the other. They were about to come to blows, when I grew nervous and closed my eyes, and instantly I heard the sound of beating. This is all that I know."

Those who devote their time to a study of Hindu society and its institutions are very much puzzled to find *Dévadasis*, a class of women consecrated to God's work, openly practising prostitution. These wretched people are required to sweep the temple, ornament the floor with quaint figures drawn in rice flour, hold before the idol the sacred light called *Kumbharati*, dance and sing when festivals are celebrated, fan the idol and do many other similar things. The word *Dévadasi* literally means servant of God, and it seems strange that a person dedicated to the service of God should lead a low and degraded life.

In Kélambakam there are two dancing girls, Kanakambujam (golden lotus) and Minakshi (fish-eyed). They are the *Dévadasis* of the temple of *Kothundarama* in the village, and they do service by turns, for which they receive an allowance from the temple endowment. Kanakambujam is the concubine of Rajaruthna Mudelliar, a burly, thick-necked zemindar of a neighbouring village, and Minakshi is in the keeping of our old friend Appalacharri, although at times the Brahmin has no scruples in acting the part of a go-between for some money consideration to those who may wish to buy his concubine's smiles. There is a good deal of what is termed "professional jealousy" between the two dancing girls, and on this account constant disputes arose between the Mudelliar and the Brahmin, which at last culminated in their being carried to a criminal court for settlement. The Mudelliar lodged a complaint with the magistrate against Appalacharri for assault and abusive language; and the Brahmin, knowing that his opponent would be cowed and willing to buy peace at any price, wantonly cited as his witnesses the zemindar's wife and aged daughter, who lived in a neighbouring village and who therefore knew nothing of the dispute. The magistrate was well aware that the action of Appalacharri was simply vexatious, and was therefore unwilling to order their appearance in court, but the clever Brahmin insisted on their being called to give evidence, as they were the only witnesses that could prove his innocence. The poor Mudelliar had in these circumstances no other alternative but to withdraw his complaint. Appalacharri is even to this day continually harassing his enemy, much to the delight of his concubine, but poor Mudelliar simply bears all this as meekly as possible.

During marriage occasions, when a number of people congregate together to witness the ceremony, Hindu females will not attend on the brides and look after them for fear of being gazed at by the people. Hence the dancing girls act the part of bridesmaids. Their duty is to dress the bride, adorn her with jewels, conduct her to the bridegroom and adjust her posture on the bridal seat. They are also required to dance and sing before the villagers on these occasions.

There is still another man in Kélambakam, who is, however, not a permanent resident of the village. He makes periodical visits to his house once a week or so, to see his wife and children. His name is Narayana Pillai, and he looks after his sheep in the plains. In my account of Gopala Pillai I gave a story illustrative of the proverbial dulness of the shepherd class. My readers will pardon me for introducing here another story to the same effect.

THE SHEPHERD AND HIS WIFE SEETA.

A shepherd youth, the dullest of his class,
Was wedded to a lovely shepherd lass;
And to her father's house the bridegroom went
To feast on all the good things for him meant.

His only cloth around his waist he wore,
His stupid head a heavy turban bore;
For once, his flock forgot, his only care,
He went to eat and to be merry there.

He thought of none but Seeta on the way,
And reached her father's house at close of day.
He entered, but the door-posts kept in check
Him and the staff that rested on his neck.

He moved, but still they kept him back, when lo!
There came, bending her head, a buffalo,
With horns as long as his own faithful staff,
And freely passed to feed upon the chaff.

Thus taught our shepherd entered in, and of
A hearty meal partook; then, heedless of his love,
Retired, and till next morning soundly slept,
While she all night her sad fate cursed, and wept.

VI.

Remarks on slavery in India—The pariahs—Mayandi, the headman of the Parcherry—The Valluvan—The chuckler—The Villee—The Korathy—The Korathy's lullaby.

THE term *slavery* conveys different ideas when considered in connection with different nations by whom it is practised. To a nation which is cold and strictly logical, which has "an unflinching courage to meet the consequences of every premise which it lays down and to work out an accursed principle, with mathematical accuracy, to its most accursed results," all the horrors of slavery so graphically and feelingly described by historians and writers of fiction may doubtless appear to be true, and all the rules of the slave code that "reduces man from the high position of a free agent, a social, religious, accountable being, down to the condition of the brute or of inanimate matter," may appear to be just. But to a nation that is "by constitution more impulsive, passionate, and poetic," those rules may appear to be illegal, unjust, and even sinful. To Hindus, who are a nation of philosophers and abstract thinkers, who give only a secondary place to the practical side of things, and who are taught by their sacred writings not to cause the least injury to even the lowest of God's creatures on pain of some dreadful punishment in a future state, slavery means a mild and perhaps an acceptable form of servitude. Hence it is that while in other countries philanthropists like Wilberforce and Theodore Parker have had to put down what has unhappily debased humanity for centuries, there exist in India even at the present day some traces of that kind of slavery which even in its worst days had no objectionable features in it. And this perhaps is owing to the peculiar characteristic of the country where agriculture forms the chief occupation of the people. In every village in Southern India will be found a parcherry in which live the *pariahs*, who in a way answer to the description of slaves in other countries.

In my previous papers, I described the persons living in the main group of buildings in Kélambakam. There is yet another group of buildings which is included in the village. It is smaller in size, and is at a distance of two or three furlongs from the main group. There are about thirty dwellings in this group, all of them thatched, and some so small that a foreigner might well stand aghast at the number of people living in them. They are built with no pretensions to order or arrangement, and each has a backyard in which are invariably to be seen tamarind, palmyra, coconut and other trees. During a good part of the year the thatched roofs are grown over with pumpkin and other vegetables, thus presenting a pleasing appearance. This group of dwellings is called the parcherry of Kélambakam, where the pariahs, the lowest class of people in Hindu society, live. There are about one hundred pariahs living here, and they are the servants of the landowners of the village. They are paid in grain. Each pariah servant in Kélambakam is paid every month at the rate of six merkals of paddy, *i.e.*, forty-eight measures. The average price of these forty-eight measures is between two and two and a half rupees (between four and five shillings). From this it will be seen that labour in South Indian villages is very cheap. For their low wages, the pariahs are required to be at their masters' bidding from early morn till the close of day. They have to plough the lands, sow paddy, water the fields, weed them, sleep in the fields when the crops are ripe, reap and thrash the corn, and do a hundred other things.

Mayandi is the headman of the parcherry of Kélambakam, and he is about eighty years of age. He served under Kothundarama Moodelly's father and grandfather. He has five sons, all grown-up men, serving under Kothundarama Moodelly and cultivating his fifty acres of land. When the pariahs have disputes to settle, they go to Mayandi for advice. Once in his youthful days some robbers entered the house of Kothundarama Moodelly's father, and with a daring and courage that were very highly spoken of at the time the pariah encountered the robbers and dispersed them. While defending his master's house from plunder, he received some very severe wounds. This incident he would relate to his sons and to the other pariahs of the village. He would show them with pride the scars on his body and ask them to follow his good example, to love their masters, and be faithful to them. Now the venerable figure of the old man may be seen in the streets of the village, and he gives glowing pictures of the days when rice was sold at twenty-four measures for one rupee, when living was cheap, when there were periodical rains, and when the lands of the village produced twice as much as they do now.

When the village is attacked with cholera, smallpox, and other pestilential diseases, the village munsiff and others in Kélambakam invariably consult old Mayandi and ask him how in former days the villagers who have passed away acted in such emergencies.

The pariahs serve the same family from generation to generation. They dare not accept service under other masters. Whenever marriages are performed in the master's house, the pariah servant gets married at the same time. For instance, when the village headman, Kothundarama Moodelly, was married, two of Mayandi's sons were also married. When a member of the master's family dies, the pariah servant and his whole household must go into mourning, and on the sixteenth day, when the funeral ceremonies are performed and the relatives of the deceased bathe in a tank, the pariah and his people go through the ceremonies and bathe in the same tank, thus showing that they are as much interested in the matter as the master. When the pariah servant is to be married, the first thing he does is to go with all his people to the master's house with fruit and flowers and obtain his permission for the marriage. When there are family disputes among the pariahs, masters are invariably consulted. From the above it will be seen that slavery in a mild form exists in Indian villages, and until quite recently what is called *Muri Sittu* (literally slavery agreement) was in vogue. But this practice of executing slavery agreements is happily fast dying out.

The pariahs are as a class hardworking, honest, and truthful. In watering the fields, in reaping the corn and in other things, they show that they are capable of very hard work. They begin at five in the morning and go on working without intermission till ten or eleven o'clock; they begin again at three in the afternoon, and do not cease till six or seven in the evening. They are honest, and zealously guard the interests of their masters. Although during the harvesting time the masters may be absent, the pariahs will not appropriate to their own use one grain of corn or take any undue advantage of their masters' absence. When the corn is ripe they sleep in the fields and honestly watch their masters' property.

They are also truthful. Lately an incident took place in Kélambakam which illustrates very well this trait in their character. Our old Brahmin friend Appalacharri was constantly quarrelling with a neighbouring landowner whose lands were being gradually encroached upon. The good-natured villager patiently bore all the aggressive acts of the Brahmin, but he was so persistently and continually harassed that he one day lost his temper and abused the Brahmin. There were present at the time two pariah servants of the villager, and Appalacharri, who was keen enough to know the truthful character of the pariahs, filed a criminal complaint against his opponent and cited the two pariahs as his witnesses. They spoke the truth and thus deposed against their own master. The poor man was punished, and Appalacharri went away successful.

The *valluvars* are the people who officiate as priests among pariahs during marriages and funerals. These people take pride in the fact that Tiruvalluvar, the reputed author of the celebrated *Kural*, was a valluvar. The valluvar of the pariahs of Kélambakam lives in a neighbouring village, and his name is Krishnan. He officiates as their priest on marriage and funeral occasions and gets a small fee for his services. He knows a little of astrology, and practises medicine in a rude form. Some years ago he was brought up before a court of sessions and was convicted for causing abortion to a woman of ill-repute.

Such are the illiterate pariahs, a unique class of men, whose pure lives and noble traits of character are in every way worthy of admiration, and whose occupation invests them with considerable importance in India, which is essentially an agricultural country.

The person next claiming our attention is Lakshmanan, the *chuckler*. He is entitled to the hides of the animals which die in the village. He prepares leather in a rough sort of way, and makes shoes, drums, &c., for the people. Lakshmanan owns an acre of land in the village which he cultivates, besides attending to his business of supplying the villagers with leather whenever they require it.

Balan, the *villee* of Kélambakam is a very interesting person. He reminds us of the naked savages of whom we often read in histories. He lives with his wife and children in a small hut at the distance of a mile from the village. He gathers honey, roots, medicinal herbs and other forest produce, which he takes to the village and exchanges for grain. He has acquired some reputation as a snake-charmer, and people from the surrounding villages go to him for scorpion and snake bites.

The marriage customs of the villee people are very curious. The bride and bridegroom sit in an open plain on a low wooden seat, surrounded by a number of their caste men. The old men among them present the couple with new clothes, and then at the appointed hour, amidst the vociferous shouting of those assembled, the bridegroom ties round the neck of the bride a string of black beads. The married persons then go round the wooden seat a number of times, after which the marriage is said to be completed. The people then sit together to eat, drink, and be merry. The name of their deity is Valleeammai, and at night a number of people join together and praise their deity in language which sounds very curious and which baffles even the most learned philologist. The villee people live mostly on leaves and roots.

Ponny is the name of the *korathy*, who goes about the villages selling mats and baskets, and, as she is also a tattooer, she might often be seen in Kélambakam offering her services for a small fee. Hindu females are very fond of having their bodies tattooed, and Ponny consequently carries on a successful trade. The korathy first makes a sketch of the figure of a scorpion or a serpent on the part of the body offered to her for tattooing, then takes a number of sharp needles, dips them in some liquid preparation which she has ready, and pricks the flesh most mercilessly. In a few days the whole appears green. This is considered a mark of beauty among the Hindus. While the tattooing takes place, the korathy sings a crude song so as to make the person undergoing the process forget the pain. The following is as nearly as possible a translation of the song which I myself heard.

THE KORATHY'S LULLABY.

Stay, darling, stay—'tis only for an hour,
And you will be the fairest of the fair.
Your lotus eyes can soothe the savage beast,
Your lips are like the newly blossomed rose,
Your teeth—they shine like pearls ; but what are they
Before the beauties of my handiwork?

Stay, darling, stay—'tis only for an hour,
And you will be the fairest of the fair.
I've left my home and all day hard I toil
So to adorn the maidens of the land
That erring husbands may return to them ;
Such are the beauties of my handiwork.

Stay, darling, stay—'tis only for an hour,
And you will be the fairest of the fair.
In days of old fair Seeta laid her head
Upon the lap of one of our own clan,
When with her lord she wandered in the wilds
And like the emerald shone her beauteous arms.

Stay, darling, stay—'tis only for an hour,
And you will be the fairest of the fair.
And often in the wilds, so it is said,
She also of the Pandus went in quest
Of one of us, but found not even one,
And sighed she was not like her sisters blest.

Stay, darling, stay—'tis only for an hour,
And you will be the fairest of the fair.
My work is done ; rejoice, for you will be
The fairest of your sisters in the land.
Rejoice for evermore, among them you
Will shine as doth the moon among the stars.

VII.

The Indian village constitution—Hindu women—A conversation among the women of the village of Kélambakam—Duriyodana's love for Subathira, and the sad result.

I HAVE in the preceding papers described the various classes of people in the village of Kélambakam. It will be seen that this village is a little world in itself, having a government of its own and preserving intact the traditions of the past in spite of the influences of a foreign government and a foreign civilization. Every member of the little state of Kélambakam regularly performs the duties allotted to him, and everything works like a machine. Those that render service for the upkeep of the village constitution are either paid in grain or have some lands allotted to them to be cultivated and enjoyed free of rent. Those that are paid in grain present themselves during the harvest time at the threshing-floor;

and when the villager gathers his corn and is ready to remove it to his house, he distributes a portion to each of the village servants, according to the nature and importance of the service rendered to him throughout the whole year. And these simple, honest villagers earn their livelihood year after year by toiling hard from early morning till the close of day, leading a peaceful and contented life, living happily with their wives and children in their humble cottage homes and caring for nothing that goes on beyond their own little village. Well has it been observed by Professor Max Müller—"To the ordinary Hindu, I mean to ninety-nine in every hundred, the village is his world, and the sphere of public opinion with its beneficial influences seldom extends beyond the horizon of his village." The doings of those who govern them and things political are nothing to them. It is enough for them if Providence blesses them with periodical rains, if their lands bring forth plenty to sustain them and their children and to preserve unruffled the quiet even tenor of their lives. This policy of non-interference and indifference to what passes outside his own sphere has been the main characteristic and, in fact, the guiding principle of the Indian villager from time immemorial, and hence arose the very familiar saying which every Hindu knows to quote, and to quote with gushing acceptance of the idea conveyed by it—"What does it matter to us, whether Rama administers the country or the Rakshasas (giants)?"

Life in Kélambakam, with its fifty or sixty dwellings inhabited by a few hundreds of people, is full of interest. The villagers get up various kinds of amusements, which bring them often together. In civilized countries, public amusements are authorized on a very grand scale; they often cost a great deal, and the best talent available is secured to please the people. But the amusements indulged in by the Indian villagers entail little or no expense, though their enjoyment derived from them is none the less keen. I shall in the following papers describe the various sports and pastimes got up by the people of Kélambakam, which now and then relieve the dull monotony of their life. But before doing so, I wish to say a few words regarding the women of the village.

In eastern countries women are said to hold

a subordinate position. The charge has often been made that in India they are bartered as slaves, that they are useful to man only in so far as they minister to his comforts, and that they are simply child-bearing machines. But European countries owe their proud position to the fact that women are honoured and respected and are accorded a superior position. There what is called love is not mere bestial passion, but something more. Such are the views thrust upon us in season and out of season by certain writers who pretend to know intimately the manners and customs of the Hindus. But the keen observer of the inner life of Hindu society will have no difficulty in discovering that the above picture is overdrawn, and that the poorest Indian villager loves his wife as tenderly and as affectionately as the most refined mortal on earth, and that in his obscure cottage, "unseen by man's disturbing eye," love shines,

> "Curtained from the sight
> Of the gross world, illumining
> One only mansion with her light."

True it is that our women do not freely mingle with the other sex, but they congregate together almost daily near such places as public wells and tanks. There they enjoy the pleasures of society as keenly as their sisters of the West and indulge in all sorts of idle talk, invariably commenting on the latest scandal of the village. The women of Kélambakam rise very early in the morning, clean their teeth, wash their faces, sweep the whole house, including even the cattle-shed, sprinkle cowdung water, ornament the floor with white powder, and then go to the temple tank to bathe. There every morning most of the females of the village meet. The temple tank in Kélambakam is a large one, and separate places for bathing are assigned to the men and the women. The women come one after another and take their accustomed places, and, during the time they wash their clothes, bathe, and attend to the usual toilette, such as putting on the red powder called *Kunkumam* and smearing the body with saffron, they freely enter into conversation, in which intelligence and wit are combined, and which will at once convince even the most superficial observer that they are not so stupid as they are sometimes represented to be. For the benefit of such of my readers as may wish to form some idea of their conversation, I shall here reproduce a conversation which took place between a number of the women of the village, and which I myself had the pleasure of overhearing.

It was a fine morning in the month of May. There was at the tank Lakshmi, the wife of the village headman Kothundarama Mudelly, usually considered the prettiest woman of the village. Though she is the happy mother of a number of children, she looked as fresh as a girl of sixteen, and it seemed as if youth and beauty were permanently settled upon her finely moulded face. There was also present Sundaram, the black ugly-looking wife of the *Kurnam*, Ramasami Pillai, but withal a good woman and a loving wife. The venerable looking old lady Seshammal, the wife of the *Purohita*, Ramanujacharri, was there, being the first to arrive at the tank. Her wrinkled face and silvery hair are doubtless the results of old age, but she was as sprightly and energetic as a young girl. She never would shrink from bathing in the tank early in the morning, even in the cold month of December.

There also were Amirtham, the wife of the schoolmaster Nalla Pillai, and the garrulous Andal, the wife of the temple *Archaka*, Varadayyangar, fat and burly looking, with thick massive features and heavy hanging arms, and ever ready to talk all sorts of scandals, especially against the good-natured Perundévi, the wife of Appalacharri, her husband's brother. There was also to be seen Thayammah, the wife of the village physician, Appasamy Vathiyar, a hard-working lady, who often took up the cudgels on behalf of Perundévi against the vexatious attacks of the scandal-loving Andal ; and there were besides these a number of other females, whose names at this distant date I do not remember. These freely entered into a conversation which lasted for some time. Perundévi, Appalacharri's wife, happened to be absent on that day for reasons which will appear from the following.

Lakshmi.—Where is that good girl Perundévi to-day ? We miss her very much.

Thayammah.—There was a good deal of noise in the Brahmin street last night, and I asked Vathiyar about it. He told me that the people in Appalacharri's house were quarrelling.

Andal.—Yes, I know all about it, but you chide me whenever I speak the truth against Perundévi.

Seshammal.—It is true there was some quarrel and the people actually came to blows. Andal knows all about it, as she takes a good deal of interest in the matter. I do not know how the dispute came about. I was then busy cooking.

Andal.—You know, Lakshmi, I told you last Monday that Appalacharri severely beat his wife, and forcibly took away from her that fine earring set with rubies which she was wearing and which we all were wont to admire. He gave the earring to his concubine Minakshi. News of this was carried to Perundévi's father's house in Conjeveram, and last night her old father, his two sons, and a number of their companions, came and questioned Appalacharri about the earring.

Amirtham.—To whom does the jewel belong?

Andal.—It was made for Perundévi by her father. She was the pet child of the family, and when she was married to Appalacharri, her people made a number of jewels for her, but none of them is so valuable as this ruby earring. Appalacharri was very badly used, but the mean fellow patiently bore all the contumely. His mother, his widowed sister, and others also came in for a good share of abuse. This, too, he quietly bore. But when one of his brothers-in-law abused Minakshi, his concubine, as being the cause of all these troubles to their beloved sister, he sprang upon the poor fellow like a tiger and severely assaulted him, saying that he would tamely submit to anything else but would never allow his dear concubine to be abused. Thereupon a free fight ensued, and Appalacharri was severely belaboured.

Sundaram.—But where is poor Perundévi now?

Andal.—They took her away to Conjeveram last night, saying that they gave away their beloved child to Appalacharri, just as a parrot, which is tenderly nursed, is given away to a cat. They swore that they would not send Perundévi back, and it is likely we shall never again enjoy her company.

Seshammal.—Oh sad fate! why should she thus suffer?

Lakshmi.—Ayyo, poor girl! Are we no more to see your beautiful face? But why is it that Appalacharri should prefer that ugly-looking concubine to the beautiful Perundévi?

Thayammah.—My husband says that Minakshi somehow administered a love potion to Appalacharri, and that is doing all the mischief. The Vathiyar is advising him every day to take medicine which will make him vomit the whole thing; then, he says, he will be all right and return to the bosom of his wife. But he will have none of it.

Lakshmi.—Stop! There comes the sinner with a face full of grief. Evidently he feels the last night's affair. Let us not speak about it.

Sundaram.—What did you prepare, Lakshmi, for your last night's meals?

Lakshmi.—A friend of my husband in Chingleput sent us a few days ago some dried brinjals of the north, and I cooked them with some dhol. The dish was so good that my husband was extremely pleased with my culinary skill. I took advantage of the occasion and reminded him of his promise to make for me a flower in gold, just like the one that Amirtham is wearing on the tuft of her hair. He promised to buy some gold immediately and send it to Conjeveram to a skilled goldsmith.

Sundaram.—Let me have some dried brinjals. I will make a nice preparation and try to please my husband.

Lakshmi.—You know they are going to read the tale called *Aniyátham* in my house this midday. I ask you all to come and hear the interesting story, and then, Sundaram, you will have some of the brinjals.

Andal.—What is the story ?

Lakshmi.—It is the story of that vile wretch Duriyodana, who, not content with depriving the Pandus of their kingdom, tried to seduce the chaste *Subathira*, the wife of Arjuna. For this he was very severely punished by Alli, the Queen of Madura.

Seshammal.—The worst sin of all is to cast a sensual eye upon another man's wife. There is a stanza in the Tamil *Prabanda* which my husband recites every day. It says that he who loves his neighbour's wife will be for ever goaded on with sharp instruments by fiends in hell to embrace the figure of a female made of red-hot iron.

Lakshmi.—That is Duriyodana's fate and he

will now be suffering for his sins. I ask you all to come to-day to my house to hear that good story.

By this time the bathing and toilet were finished, and they all returned to their homes. According to the invitation, they again met at about one o'clock to hear the story of *Aniyátham* read. The author of the poem, which is in Tamil, is Pugazhenthi, a well-known poet who lived in Madura about the tenth or eleventh century, when the Pandyan kings were the rulers of the country. When the daughter of his king was married to a Chola king, the poet accompanied the bride to the Chola court as a part of her dowry. The poets there grew envious of the new-comer and got him imprisoned. It was while in prison that our poet composed the tale called *Aniyátham* and many other similar works. The story runs that he used to recite his tales to the women of the town, who had to pass by the prison to a neighbouring tank for water, and that they in turn made his prison life comfortable by throwing fruits and cakes into his cell. The works of Pugazhenthi are even to this day very popular with the women of the country. The following is a brief outline of the story called *Aniyátham.*

When the Pandus lost their kingdom and in fact their everything in gambling, it was stipulated that they should live in the wilderness for a number of years. This they did, and Duriyodana, their half-brother, who had long wished to seduce Subathira, the wife of Arjuna, wanted to take advantage of their absence in the wilderness and go to Madura, where the fair lady was living. Duriyodana first laid the matter before his own minister, who was quite against the proposal. Then he went to his own wife and said—" My dear wife, lands and riches I have, and this fair world encompassed by the vast ocean is at my feet. But there is one thing wanting to complete my joy. I have set my heart upon brave Arjuna's wife. She now lives with Alli, the Queen of Madura. Permit me, therefore, to go to the banks of the Vaigai to effect my purpose." His wife advised him not to take such a serious step, and implored him to stay. But heedless of the good advice of his wife and his wise minister, he went to Madura and submitted his proposal to the Queen of that place. But that brave

Queen, wishing to punish the man who made such a nefarious request, sent word to say that Subathira would be sent with him if he would come again in a few days. In the meantime the Queen of Madura sent for some carpenters and got a curious ladder made. It was so constructed that any one ascending it would necessarily get nailed to it, and both man and ladder would straightway fly in the air. Duriyodana returned to Madura in a few days as directed, and requested the Queen to send Subathira with him. The Queen replied that his request would be complied with on his ascending a ladder which was in her possession. To this he consented, and such was his love for the beautiful wife of Arjuna that he immediately began to ascend the ladder. And what was the result? He and the ladder were both seen flying in the air by Athisesha, by Indra, by the five Pandus, and by all the world. The people laughed at him, and he was reduced to such extremities that he requested the Queen of Madura to extricate him from his perilous position. He was at last set free, and was thus taught not to love his neighbour's wife.

VIII.

The village bards—The story of the royal huntress.

MACAULAY says: "The Greek Rhapsodists, according to Plato, could scarce recite Homer without falling into convulsions. The Mohawk hardly feels the scalping knife while he shouts his death song. The power which the ancient bards of Wales and Germany exercised over their auditors seems to modern readers almost miraculous." The above remark applies with equal force to the Indian bards, who go about in villages reciting tales. The power exercised by them over the villagers is simply marvellous. I once witnessed two bards reciting a tale to the people of Kélambakam, wherein the adventures of a royal prince, his adversity, his banishment from the land of his fathers, his love for a huntress, and his ultimate marriage with her, were all graphically described. The following is the story. It first describes the land over which a good king ruled.

It was a land of plenty and of wealth ;
There God's indulgent hand made for a race
Supremely blest a paradise on earth.
A land of virtue, truth, and charity,
Where nature's choicest treasures man enjoyed
With little toil, where youth respected age,
Where each his neighbour's wife his sister deemed,
Where side by side the tiger and the lamb
The water drank, and sported oft in mirth.
A land where each man deemed him highly blest
When he relieved the mis'ries of the poor,
When to his roof the wearied traveller came
To share his proffered bounty with good cheer.
Such was the far famed land of Panchala.

The good king is then described in the following lines.

Here reigned a king who walked in virtue's path,
Who ruled his country only for his God.
His people's good he deemed his only care,
Their sorrows were his sorrows, and their joys
He counted as his own ; such was the king
Whose daily prayers went up to Him on high
For wisdom and for strength to rule his men
Aright, and guard the land from foreign foes.
Such was the far famed king of Panchala.

This good king had a son who is next spoken of in the tale.

An only son he had—a noble prince,
The terror of his foes, the poor man's friend.
He mastered all the arts of peace and war,
And was a worthy father's worthy son.
What gifts and graces men as beauties deem,
These nature freely lavished on the youth,
And people loved in wonder to behold
The face that kindled pleasure in their minds.
The courage of a warrior in the field,
A woman's tender pity to the weak,
All these were centred in the royal youth.
His arrows killed full many a beast that wrought
Dread havoc on the cattle of the poor.
Such was the famous prince of Panchala.

Then follows an account of the good people of the country. They go to their king and complain to him of a ferocious tiger.

The people, they were all true men and good,
Their ruler they adored, for by their God
He was ordained to rule their native land.
They freely to their king made known their wants,
And he as freely satisfied their needs,
And e'en the meanest of the land deemed it
The basest act to sin against his king.
Such were the people of the ancient land
Of Panchala, who stood one day with tears
Before their king to pour their plaintive tales
Of ruin wrought upon their cattle by
The tiger of the forest, that all day
Was safe in his impenetrable lair,
But every night his dreaded figure showed
And feasted on the flesh of toiling beasts.

8

The king at once commands his son to go to the forest and kill the beast.

> The king gave ear to their sad tales of woe,
> And straightway called his only son, and said—
> "Dear son! my people's good I value more
> Than thine own life. Go therefore to the woods
> With all thine arrows and thy trusty bow,
> And drag the dreaded tiger from his den,
> And to their homes their wonted peace restore.
> His spotted skin and murderous claws must soon
> Be added to the trophies of the past,
> Now hanging on our ancient palace walls."

The prince obeys his father, but for a while his search for the tiger proves fruitless.

> The prince obeyed, and to the forest went,
> Three days and nights he wandered in the woods,
> But still found not the object of his search.
> He missed his faithful men and lost his way,
> Till worn and weary underneath a tree,
> Whose shady boughs extended far and wide,
> The lonely straggler stretched his limbs and slept,
> And for a time forgot his dire distress.

The prince's feelings are then very graphically described in the following lines.

> He woke, and thus addressed himself with tears,
> "Here I am left deserted and alone;
> Perchance my faithful people at this hour,
> Are vainly searching for their hapless prince,
> While I die here of hunger and of thirst.

And gladly would I welcome now the brute
That has attracted me to this strange spot,
To plunge his claws into my body, tear
My flesh, and break my bones, and feast on me
By gnawing them between his horrid jaws,
And so spare me from this slow lingering death."

The prince then meets a huntress, and the meeting is thus related.

So thought the royal youth of his sad doom,
When lo! a spotless figure, with a bow,
A pouch with arrows dangling on her back,
A hatchet in her hand for cutting wood,
And with a pitcher on her head, appeared.
Here every day she came to gather wood,
And, dressed in male attire, her heavy load
Took to the nearest town, sold it, then reached,
At close of day to cook the ev'ning meal,
Her cottage on the outskirts of the wood,
Where, with her sire, bent down with years, she lived,
And dragged her daily miserable life.
Such was the maid that was upon that day,
As if by instinct, drawn to the fair youth,
And such the huntress Radha he beheld.
A fairer woman never breathed the air,
No, not in all the land of Panchala.

They meet, and the prince subsequently kills the tiger with the help of the huntress, who gives him food.

The maid in pity saw his wretched plight,
Then from the pitcher took her midday meal,

And soon relieved his hunger and his thirst.
The grateful prince, delighted, told his tale,
And she, well pleased, thus spake—"Fair youth! grieve not,
Behold the brook that yonder steals along,
To this the tiger comes at noon to quench
His thirst. Then, safely perched upon a tree,
We can for ever check his deadly course."
Both went, and saw at the expected hour
The monarch of the forest near the brook.
In quick succession, lightning-like from them
The arrows flew, and in a moment fell
His massive body lifeless on the ground.

The king's son then takes leave of the huntress, and returns home.

Then vowing oft to meet his valiant friend,
The prince returned, and with the happy news
Appeared before the king, who blest his son
And said: "My son! well hast thou done the deed;
Thy life thou hast endangered for my men;
Ask anything and I will give it thee."
"I want not wealth nor power," the prince replied,
"But, noble father! one request I make.
I chanced to meet a huntress in the wood,
And Radha is her name; she saved my life.
I but for her had died a lingering death,
Her valour and her beauty I admire,
And therefore grant me leave to marry her."

The father resents this request, and banishes the prince from the country.

The king spake not, but forthwith gave command
To banish from his home the reckless youth,
Who brought disgrace upon his royal house,
And who, he wished, should wed one worthy of
The noble race of ancient Panchala.
Poor youth ! he left his country and his home,
He that was dreaded by his foes was gone.

The neighbouring king, taking advantage of the prince's absence from the country, invades Panchala.

Vain lust of power impelled the neighb'ring king,
The traitor who usurped his sovereign's throne,
To march on Panchala with all his men.
He went, and to the helpless king proclaimed—
"Thou knowest well my armies are the best
On earth, and folly it will be in thee
To stand 'gainst them and shed thy people's blood.
Send forth thy greatest archer, and with him
My prowess I will try ; this will decide,
If you or I should sit upon the throne,
And whether Panchala is thine or mine."
The king, bewildered, knew not what to do,
But soon two maidens, strangers to the land,
Met him, and, of the two, the younger said—
" O righteous king ! we left our distant homes
To visit shrines and bathe in holy streams.
We have been wandering in many climes,
And yesternight this place we reached, and heard
Your loyal people speak of your sad plight.
In early youth I learned to use the bow,
I pray thee, therefore, send me forth against
The wretch that dares to wrest this land from thee."

The king was pleased with this offer, which he gladly accepted. He sent word to the invader, and the hour and place of the contest were named. The contending parties duly met.

> And ere the treacherous wretch could string his bow,
> A pointed arrow, carrying death with it,
> Like lightning flew from forth the maiden's hands,
> Pierced deep into his head, that plans devised
> To kill his royal master and once more
> Thought ill of Panchala and her good king.
> His body lifeless lay upon the field.

The king was highly pleased with the victor, and asked her to state whatever request she had to make. Thereupon, the brave woman replied as follows :—

> " Thou, noble ruler of this ancient land !
> Before thy sacred presence and before
> All these assembled in thy royal court,
> I will reveal my story, sad but true.
> I am the only child of him that ruled
> The neighbouring state, whose kings for centuries
> In peace and friendship lived with Panchala.
> Alas ! the villain, whom my arrow gave
> To crows and to the eagles of the air,
> Usurped my father's throne, and, sad to tell,
> He instant orders gave to murder us.
> The menials sent to do the cruel deed
> Felt pity for the fallen king and me,

His only daughter, in the woods left us
And went away, reporting they had done
The deed ; and there, in that deserted place,
Unknown we lived a wretched life for years.
And glad I am that death ignoble, which
The wretch deserved, has now befallen him.
This person standing here—I now remove
The veil, and, by the mole upon his breast,
Behold in him thine own begotten son—
Was by thy orders banished from the land.
Grant that I now may plead for him, because
A woman's words can sooner soothe the heart.
I crave your Majesty to pardon him
For loving me, and take him back unto
His father's home ; grant also, gracious king,
That I, a princess, may be worthy deemed
Of being wedded to thine only son."

The king, rejoiced at this, immediately issued orders for the marriage of the prince and the princess. The story goes on to tell how they in their turn ruled a double kingdom for many long years.

IX.

Jugglers and acrobats—Introductory remarks—An account of the several feats performed by the jugglers and acrobats.

THE months of January, February, and March are pleasant months to the Indian villager and his hard-working cattle. In Southern India, agricultural operations commence about the month of July. As soon as the lands are in a fit condition, the villager takes his cattle to plough his fields, and the ploughing usually occupies several days. Then at the proper times, which he knows by experience, he sows the paddy, attends to the weeding and anxiously looks up to the sky for the periodical rains, and, if they fail, waters the fields from a neighbouring well. The water has to be lifted up at times from a depth of fifteen or twenty feet. This process of irrigation is both difficult and laborious. The villager goes to the well with two others as early as three or four o'clock in the morning and goes on drawing water till nine ; he again commences work at three in the afternoon, and does not stop till it gets dark, and oftentimes, if it is a moonlight night, continues till eight or nine o'clock. It will thus be seen that the villager, whenever occasion requires, does not shrink from working for even twelve or thirteen hours a day. All this time, he cheers himself by singing enlivening songs. Singing songs when fields are watered has become a regular institution in the country, and Hindu women, who pass by, invariably stop to hear the songs, and catch with avidity everything that comes from the lips of the singer. From what they hear in this way they often divine future events. For about the space of five long months, the Indian villager tenderly nurses the plants, as he would his own children, watches their progress day after day with "contending hopes and fears," and even when the corn gets ripe his anxiety does not cease. He then denies to himself the pleasure of sleeping in his own house. He constructs for himself a temporary bed in the midst of his fields, and there, regardless of the piercing cold or venomous reptiles, keeps his nightly watch to prevent other people's cattle from committing mischief, to scare away birds that constantly light in numbers on the fields to pick up the grain, and to look after light-fingered gentlemen who find it convenient to carry on their avocations at night. About the end of December or the beginning of January the harvest commences. Then, with thankfulness to God, he stores in his granary the hard-earned grain, which is to sustain him, his wife, and children for a whole year, and in the backyard of his house heaps the straw, for the use of the cattle, that shared with him the hard toil of the previous months. Then comes a period of rest. The anxiety of the villager is now over and he has no cares to occupy his thoughts, and naturally yearns after amusements. It is about this time and the succeeding months of April, May, and June, when the heat is somewhat unbearable, that marriages and other festivals are generally celebrated by him.

One cool morning about the end of January, when man and beast were at ease, and the people of Kélambakam, having little to do, were longing for some amusement to while away their time, a cluster of people were basking in the sun and spending their time in idle gossip. Muthu Naick, the village watchman, came and informed Kothundarama Mudelly, who formed one of the company, that a troupe of jugglers and acrobats had come to Kélambakam the previous evening and were encamped in the fine mango tope near the temple tank. The whole village was soon in a bustle, as the news spread like wildfire. Little urchins ran to their mothers to tell the glad news, and some even ran to the mango grove to see the new-comers. The women of the village, young and old, were all on the tip-toe of expectation, and commenced to prepare the midday meal earlier than usual.

The jugglers who came to Kélambakam that day belonged to the Thombarava caste. The Thombaravas are a nomad class of people, who earn their livelihood by wandering about the country and exhibiting their feats. The troupe consisted of the chief man, who was about forty years of age, his wife, who was between twenty-five and thirty, his brother, a strong, muscular, well-built youth of twenty, and his two little boys aged about nine and seven. The principal man came to the village munsiff and begged permission to exhibit his feats and show his skill before all the people of the village. After consultation with the chief men of the place permission was at once granted, and it was decided that the performance should commence at three in the afternoon. Long before the appointed hour, the people of the village, young and old, and even pariahs from the parcherry, flocked into the open space opposite to Kothundarama Mudelly's house and anxiously waited to witness the exhibition. The headman and the more respectable people were seated on mats before the performers. The rest of the people stood surrounding the performers, who had sufficient space in the middle to exhibit their feats. The females were standing in a group in a separate place, and some young men actually climbed up a tree that was near and were safely perched on the branches. The headman having given permission for the performance to commence, the chief juggler took his drum and began to beat it violently. Its discordant notes were heard far and wide, and the result was that more people came running to the spot. It might be safely said that most of the people of Kélambakam were present on the occasion. The juggler than said—"Great and good men of Kélambakam! I have performed my most astounding feats to the admiration of all that have seen them. I have performed before the Zemindar Runga Reddy, and he was pleased to present me with a laced cloth. I showed my extraordinary skill in jugglery to Zemindar Ramasamy Mudelly, and he was pleased to make a present of the new cloth which my wife is now wearing; and only yesterday I played before the people of the neighbouring village, who were so well pleased with me that they gave me money, old clothes, and abundance of grain. But I know you are even more liberal than all these. I pray that you will witness my great feats and reward me as I deserve." So saying, he asked his brother and his two little boys to step forward. They came and bowed to the audience and then made a number of somersaults, double and single. These were done by all the three in quick succession.

Then the two little boys came forward and lay down, the one upon the other. They rolled on the ground with such singular swiftness that soon the outlines of their bodies were entirely lost to the eye, and they looked like a cannon-ball rolling on the ground. This little feat excited the highest admiration of the audience, and the little ones at once became the favourites of the villagers, who, as will be seen afterwards, showed their appreciation in a tangible form.

The third item in the programme was even more wonderful than the above. The chief man brought a coconut and asked some of the audience to examine it. He said that his brother would throw it into the air, and that, falling upon the crown of his head, it would break in two. So saying, he gave the coconut to the youth, who examined it and threw it up to a height of about fifteen feet, but instead of fearlessly holding up his head, slipped aside, pretending to be afraid to undergo the dangerous ordeal. The principal performer, then patting the youth on the back, said that he should not be so mindful of his life, that the good will and approbation of the good people of Kélambakam were more to them than his life, and that therefore he should not shrink from performing the dangerous feat. Thus admonished, the youth once more took the coconut, threw it up, and stood upright like a column without wavering for a single instant. The coconut came down upon the crown of his head, and straightway fell to the ground in two pieces. Soon there arose a shout among the people who witnessed this extraordinary feat. Some said "Shabash!" some said that they had not see the like before, and Kothundarama Mudelly and others showed a desire to examine the youth's head. But nothing was visible there. His head was as sound as ever it had been.

The next thing shown was the *mango tree trick.* The chief actor took a mango seed, showed it to the people, and then planted it in the ground. He sprinkled some water over it and covered it with a basket. A few minutes afterwards he took out the basket, and lo! there was found a tender plant with two or three leaves sprouting out of the seed. More water was poured over it, and it was again covered with a basket. After the lapse of a few minutes more the plant was found in fresh growth with a height of about ten or twelve inches. The same process was repeated three or four times, and on the last occasion the plant rose to a height of three or four feet. Thus in the short space of half an hour the mango seed became a tree. This trick is very common in this country, and it is said that jugglers even cause fruit to grow and distribute it to the people. Our juggler was not able to do this, as mango trees bear fruit only in May and June, and this performance took place in January.

After this came a dangerous and difficult feat. The chief performer, planting his feet close together, stood in the middle of the ring like a column. His brother then climbed over his body with great agility, stood upon his shoulders, and lifted up one of the two boys, who, resting his hands upon the crown of his uncle's head, raised his legs into the air. In that perilous position, he performed some clever feats, which the people beheld with wonder and not without a sense of fear for the safety of the small performer. This was considered as simply marvellous from the way the people showed their appreciation of this exhibition of skill on the part of the boy, but what would they say to the following, described in the autobiography of the Mogul Emperor, Jehanghir? "One of seven men," says the Emperor, "stood upright before us, a second passed upwards, along his body, and head to head placed his feet upwards in the air. A third managed to climb up in the same manner, and, planting his feet on those of the second, stood with his head upwards, and so alternately to the seventh, who crowned this marvellous human pillar with his head uppermost. And what excited an extraordinary clamour of surprise was to observe the first man, who thus supported upon the crown of his head the whole of the other six, lift one foot as high as his shoulder, standing thus upon one leg and exhibiting a degree of strength and steadiness not exactly within the scope of my comprehension."

The next scene enacted was the *needle trick.* A needle, such is ordinarily used by the people, was placed on the ground with the point turned upwards. The female performer walked on her hands, and reached the place where the needle was planted. Then gently lowering herself, she lifted the needle with her eye by skilfully closing the lids on the point. This wonderful feat was greatly admired by the simple villagers, and Appalacharri was loud in his praises of the woman's skill.

The chief man then took a cannon-ball about the size of a large-sized wood-apple, and asked the people to examine it and note its weight. He threw it to a height of fifteen or twenty feet, and adjusted himself in such a way that the ball fell on the nape of his neck. Then he made certain motions of the body with extreme agility, and the ball swiftly rolled on his back in all directions and even right along each arm.

Then a block of granite that was lying in a corner of the street was brought by four villagers into the ring. It was about a yard in length, three-fourths of a foot in breadth, and about half a foot in height. Strong ropes were passed round both ends of the granite block and tied to the flowing hair of the second performer. Thus fastened, the stone was lifted from the ground by four men, who afterwards let it go. Forthwith the youth, with his heavy weight, whirled round and round, and soon the man and the stone were lost to the eye. The people of the village were loud in their praises of this herculean feat.

After this, about six or seven earthen pots, of various sizes, were placed one above the other on the head of the chief performer, so that they resembled a conical pillar. Skilfully balancing the weight on his head, the juggler climbed up a bamboo pole about twenty feet high, which was firmly planted in the ground. Then, closely fixing his legs to the bamboo and steadily holding its end in his grip, he commenced to move backwards and forwards. The bending capacity of the bamboo pole was very great, and the utmost limits were reached on either side, so that this feat, apart from its difficult nature, presented a most interesting sight to the beholders. As soon as the performer got down, they found, to their great astonishment, that the pots remained intact, and that their positions were not in the least changed.

The last, but not the least, of the performances which formed a most fitting close to this varied and interesting programme, was *the strange disappearance scene.* The woman was brought forward, and her legs and feet were tied together with a strong rope. She was then put into a basket, which was afterwards covered. After a little while the basket was opened and was found empty. The woman was not there. By and by the husband called the missing woman by her name, which she answered to from a corner of the street. This closed the performance, and the people were extremely delighted with the whole thing. Some gave old clothes to the performers, and others made presents in money. The women of the village vied with the men in rewarding the actors, and they took especial delight in giving the two boys cakes and other eatables. Our old friend Appalacharri gave the woman an old cloth and some money also, and, by the orders of the village headman, every household in the village gave half a measure of paddy.

Thus ended a pleasant afternoon's amusement. It formed the subject of the daily talk in Kélambakam for several days, and for months afterwards the people had a vivid recollection of this visit of the jugglers to the village.

X.

Snake-charmers and animal-tamers—Hindu feeling regarding the serpent—The snake-charmer and his feats—The highly intelligent cows and bullocks.

MEN in the ruder stages of civilization often regard the lower animals as objects of worship. Some animals rouse feelings of hatred and fear; some are regarded with affection and gratitude on account of their usefulness to man; and others induce a feeling of awe and admiration on account of the remarkable powers of intelligence which they display. Many animals have in India been deemed worthy of adoration. The snake is worshipped because it is dreaded. For the cow the Hindu has the highest veneration. It is a tame, innocent animal, and its usefulness to man is of the highest kind. The milk and its different products form the most valuable staple of human consumption in this country. People love this most useful animal, feel grateful to it for the various benefits it confers on them, and therefore worship it. Then, again, the monkey is adored for its superior intelligence. Animal worship in this country is accordingly traceable to the above three causes.

First, then, as regards the serpent. It is not in India alone, but in other countries also that such objects as are feared and detested have come to be worshipped by man, thus exemplifying the truth of the old saying, "Fear made the first gods in the world" (*Primos in orbe deos fecit timor*). The snake is the most dreaded animal in this country. We find mention made of it largely in our ancient writings. The dreadful effects of snake-poison used in instruments of war are vividly described in the *Ramayana*, wherein we find the warrior Lakshmana lying senseless on the field on account of the poisonous arrows used by Ravana's son. In the story of Harichandra, with which every Hindu is familiar, we read of Harichandra's only son having been bitten by a snake, and that was considered to be the greatest misfortune that could have befallen him. In the story of Nala, another very popular story, we read that queen Thamayanthi was in her troublous days devoured by a huge serpent in the desert. Again, it is one of the principal beliefs of the Hindu that *Adisésha*, the thousand-headed snake, supports the earth. Vishnu, the preserving power of the Hindu trinity, is said to sleep upon the serpent, and Siva, the destroying power, wears it as an ornament. It is the vulgar belief that eclipses are caused by the serpent. This dreaded reptile has given occasion to a good many common sayings. There is a saying in Tamil to the effect that the sight of a snake is enough to strike terror into a whole army. Another says that a serpent that is found in the midst of even ten persons is not in any danger of being killed. Such is the fear with which it is regarded. Is it any wonder, then, that people adore it? When a snake is killed, the Hindu performs ceremonies similar to those performed in honour of a dead relative. Again, people go to places which are said to be the haunts of these venomous reptiles on a particular day of the year, and there pour out milk. The dancing girl is said to be an adept in her profession if, with a serpent round her neck, she fearlessly dances before an assembly.

From the above it will be seen that a good deal of importance is attached to this reptile, and that it is largely mixed up with our beliefs and superstitions; so much so, that it has become man's highest effort to devise means to charm this animal. Snake-charming is a very ancient art in India, for we read that snake-charmers were found in this country in the days of Alexander the Great. Now-a-days snake-charmers are to be found going about the country and gaining an easy and comfortable living.

Kélambakam was one day visited by a snake-charmer. He wore a large turband (head-dress) and a charmed armlet, made of copper, which is said to exercise considerable influence on serpents and make them do as he pleases. In one hand he had a pipe made of the dried shell of the Indian gourd with a bamboo reed inserted in it, and in the other a small basket. The snake-charmer's pipe is called *Magadi*, and it is said that the music of this instrument has a peculiar attraction for snakes. Such was the paraphernalia of the man who visited

Kélambakam, and who of course first went to the house of Kothundarama Mudelly and played on his instrument. Instantly the head-man and thc inmates of the house, as also a number of people from the neighbouring houses, came to the spot to see the charmer exhibiting his snakes. He said, "Good and noble men, I have in this basket four large cobras, one of which is a black cobra, the most ferocious of all. Any moment they would surely bury their poisonous fangs in my body, but by this charmed armlet I am protected; and when once I strip myself of it, I lose all control over them; though even if they bite me I am not afraid, for I have now in my possession a most efficacious medicine which, when used on the part bitten, at once absorbs the poison. I will show you instantly how these dangerous animals appreciate my music, and you will also see the black cobra kiss me." So saying, he again began to blow the pipe for some time; then carefully opencd the basket, and out came four large cobras, and, spreading their hoods, began to move to and fro. The snakes turned their hoods whichever way he turned the hand on which he had the armlet. By this he wanted to convince the spectators of the wonderful influence which the armlet had over them. Then carefully placing all the cobras except the black one in his basket, he again played on the pipe. This time, it seemed, he took greater care in playing on his instrument. The black cobra raised its hood higher and higher as he went on playing on the pipe and approaching it nearer and nearer. Then, as he suddenly stopped the music, the cobra made a hissing noise and put down its head, and in doing so slightly touched the charmer's lips. The people beheld with wonder this black cobra kiss the charmer—this venomous reptile which could in a few seconds kill him. They were highly satisfied with his skill in snake-charming, and put to him a thousand and one questions regarding snakes generally. Then he offered for sale the medicine which he had for snake poison. Every household in the village took care to buy some of it, and safely treasured it in their house. They had implicit confidence in the efficacy of the medicine, of which, they said, only he was the happy possessor. This snake-charmer is pretty well known in and about Kélambakam, and he is also constantly seen at fairs and festivals, exhibiting his snakes and selling his medicines.

There is another class of people in Southern India who educate cows and bullocks, which they train to such a high degree of perfection that even animal tamers in European countries would be taken with surprise. Two people once came to our village. One was in charge of a fine-looking bull named Rama, and the other was in charge of a cow, a very fine specimen of her kind. She was named Seeta. The bull, which was adorned with metal bells and other ornaments, was first brought before the people, and a number of questions were put to him by the man in charge. "Are we in a village whose people are generous and willing in bestowing rewards upon worthy men?" said he. At this the bull shook his head, and the people at once understood him to answer in the affirmative. To questions that required a negative answer the bull remained motionless, and to questions that required answers in the affirmative the bull shook his head. Then said the man to the bull, "Now point out the headman of the village, whose generous disposition and whose liberality is in the mouth of every one." On this the animal, followed by the man in charge, forthwith walked up to Kothundarama Mudelly. The villagers derived great amusement and pleasure from this exhibition of the animal's intelligence. Then was performed a most interesting scene. The man in charge of Seeta went up to her, and told her that Rama, her husband, unmindful of his lawfully wedded wife, had on the previous day bestowed his affections upon another. The cow, on hearing this, turned away from her husband, and refused to follow him. The man in charge went to her, and by smooth words tried to dissuade her from taking such an unfortunate step. The cow was inexorable. Then the bullock was requested to go to his wife and amicably settle their dispute; but he was equally unyielding. At last the man in charge of the cow went near and said, "Good Seetamma! it won't do for you to persist in your folly. It is not right, nor is it according to the Shastras, that your husband should come to you and ask your pardon. Come, therefore, and be reconciled to your husband." The cow resented this request of the mediator, and showed her anger by running against him as if to gore him. After a time the matter was settled by the cow of her own accord going to her husband and kneeling before him. Rama, the bullock, was satisfied, and both walked side by side, while the two people in charge of the animals beat their drums in celebration of the happy union of a pair that had been unfortunately separated by a painful incident, though for a short time. The villagers were simply delighted with the performance of these highly-trained animals, and they showed their appreciation of the performance by giving the animals oil-cakes and other things to eat and the two persons presents in grain and old clothes.

XI.

The village preacher—His sermon on the incident related in the Mahabaratha, viz., *Sindhava's Death*.

> "And oft at night when ended was their toil,
> The villagers with souls enraptured heard him
> In fiery accents speak of Krishna's deeds
> And Rama's warlike skill, and wondered that
> He knew so well the deities they adored."

THE two great national epics of India, the *Ramayana* and the *Mahabarata*, have in every age charmed their readers and powerfully exerted their ennobling influence on the character and modes of thought of the people of this country. This is partly owing to the fact that they have intrinsic merit of their own, as being the grandest literary achievements of India's master minds, and in a great measure owing to the strong conviction that they are *Thévakathas* (stories of God). Hence they have a powerful hold on the minds of a people who are known to be extremely religious, who are taught to believe by their sacred writings that to hear or read the divine stories is to secure the path to heaven, and whose whole effort in thought and action has been directed towards the attainment of perpetual beatitude after death. No other work in India at the present day possesses the attraction which these epics have for the majority of the people. The pious Hindu will walk great distances, will sit up for hours and will be ready to forego all sorts of conveniences, if he only gets an opportunity to hear these divine stories, though it may be for the hundredth time. Various ways are devised to entertain the people with the stirring incidents of the *Ramayana* and the *Mahabarata*. They are produced on the stage in the form of plays, they are recited by professional bards in lyric verse, and they are expounded to the public in plain prose. No wonder therefore that professional preachers are found everywhere in the country, even in obscure villages, who sermonize on the popular incidents to be found in the *Ramayana* and the *Mahabarata*, and that willing ears are ever found ready to listen to them and help them to gain an easy and comfortable living.

In Kélambakam, the preacher who delights its inhabitants is Nalla Pillai, the schoolmaster. He has read very carefully all the fourteen thousand stanzas of his great-grandfather's *Mahabarata* in Tamil, and at night in the summer season, when the villagers have nothing to do, he explains them to the people. His fame as a preacher is pretty well established, and people from the neighbouring villages attend his preaching. I myself had once the pleasure and privilege of hearing this preacher of Kélambakam, and I will here give what fell from his lips, word for word. People came pouring in from Kélambakam and from neighbouring villages to the house of the village headman. On the pial of his house was seated the preacher. Before him was placed the picture of Krishna playing the flute and leaning on a cow. The picture was profusely decorated with flowers. There were also two small vessels. In one there were camphor and some burning incense, in the other were flowers and fruits. The people swarmed about like bees. Some were seated in the open street, and others on the pials of the neighbouring houses, the whole audience being eager to catch the words that fell from the preacher's lips. At eight o'clock, the preaching commenced. The moon was shining over the motley crowd who had assembled to hear the doings of their favourite deity. There was dead silence. The camphor was first lighted and incense burnt. The preacher knelt down before the picture, and then seating himself commenced to speak. The story related by him that night was *Sindhava's Death*. He said :—

"Great and noble men! Yesterday I recounted to you the wondrous deeds of Abhimanna, the worthy son of Arjuna, by his wife Subhadra, Krishna's sister. I told you how this young lion of the Pandus, this worthy son of his worthy father, fought against great odds in the field of battle, killing with his destructive arrows his enemies by thousands and tens of thousands. I told you how, like a brand thrown on a huge heap of dried grass, he committed havoc on the enemy's camp. Like the morning sun rising in all his glory, he went forth to battle to fight, and as the bright rays of that luminary, as he ascends the meridian sky, grow fiercer and fiercer, so grew the courage of this young warrior. The fiercer the battle, the greater was the courage shown by him in the field of battle. He pierced the invulnerable army of the enemy. He broke the lotus formation, killed thousands of thousands of huge elephants and mettled horses; he disabled the strongly built chariots of the enemy and gave to crows and eagles those who dared to oppose him. Blood flowed like water, and the havoc committed among the enemy's forces was tremendous. Mangled corpses of gaily decked warriors and richly caparisoned elephants and horses, lay thickly strewn on that field of battle. The enemy was terror-stricken, and for a time knew not what to do. When Abhimanna went into the midst of the army arranged like the lotus, he was hemmed in on all sides by the hostile forces. He fought against great odds and his chariot was disabled. On foot he fought, sending destruction and death to the right of him, to the left of him, in front of him, and behind him—so that even the boldest warrior in the hostile camp was afraid to approach this young lion. The work of destruction was awful. But the surging mass still pressed against him, and he was unable to extricate himself from his perilous position.

This skilled warrior pierced deep into the army, and went into the midst of the lotus formation; but was unable to return to his ranks. I will tell you how it was that he failed to return victorious to his father. During the last months of Subhadra's pregnancy, when Abhimanna was in his mother's womb, our saviour Krishna, who is related to her as brother, was one night describing to her, to while away her time, the arts of war, and was vividly explaining how the different formations of the army such as *Pathmavyugam* (lotus formation), *Sakatavyugam* (chariot formation), *Magaravyugam* (fish formation) are constructed. While he was explaining to her the *Pathmavyugam*, she fell asleep. The child in the womb was carefully attending to what was being said by Krishna, who came to know that the mother was asleep, and that the child was hearing him on behalf of the mother, just when he finished his explanation of the lotus construction. There he stopped, and unfortunately did not explain how the same construction should be broken. Thus it was that poor Abhimanna, who went into the very midst of the lotus, did not know how to get out again. He was in great straits, and as a last resource took out his conch shell and blew it with all his might so that its warning voice might apprise his father of his dangerous position. At this juncture Krishna purposely blew his conch shell in another part of the field, and thereby drowned the sound that issued from Abhimanna's shell. Thus poor Abhimanna, hemmed in on all sides, fell on the field of battle, slain by Sindhava, the brave ruler of the Sindhus. Like the morning sun he went forth in all his glory to the field of battle; like the meridian sun he fought fiercely, sending his scorching arrows and killing all that dared to oppose him; and like the setting sun sinking into the western ocean, his corpse fell down in the ocean of blood that flowed from the bodies of the elephants, horses, and fighting warriors, killed by his arrows. What a sad fall there was, when the noblest and the bravest of the Pandava army fell fighting alone in the field of battle!

"News of Abhimanna's sad death was carried to the Pandava army that very night; but human tongue cannot express the inexpressible grief with which his father, the high-souled Arjuna, was afflicted! He wept, beat his breast, and bit his lips. He brought to his memory the beauteous form of his late beloved son, his prowess and his skill in war, and he sobbed and wept. His brother-in-law Krishna tried to console him, but he refused to be consoled, saying that the loss he had sustained was irreparable. Krishna said: 'Thou noble Dhananjaya! Why should a Kshatriya and a warrior such as thou art weep like a child, weep for him, who, like one worthy of his martial race, died in the field of battle facing the enemy? He is now in *Viraswarga*, that abode in heaven where warriors dying in battle enjoy for ever God's presence. You should be proud of such a son; why then grieve for him?' These words had no effect upon the sorrow-stricken father, who still questioned his men as to how his son fought in battle, what armies he routed and who in the end killed him; and when he was told that Sindhava, the ruler of the Sindhus and Duriyodhana's brother-in-law, was the cause of his dear son's death, his sorrow was suddenly turned to anger, and in the presence of Krishna, of his own brothers, and of his assembled men, he vowed vengeance on the man who slew his son. 'If by to-morrow evening,' he exclaimed, 'before the setting of the sun, I do not, with this my *gandiba*, kill the slayer of my son, that wretch who slew a young child, and brought on me all this misery, that sinner for whom the worst part of hell is reserved—if before the setting of the sun to-morrow I do not kill him, I will throw myself on the burning pyre and be consumed to ashes. Be witness to this my vow, O mother earth, ye spirits of the firmament, and all ye gods! my faithful *gandiba* that hast through all my life so faithfully assisted me, be thou also a witness! If I do not keep this vow, the worst part of hell shall be reserved for me. That place in Yama's abode which is set apart for him that killed a thousand Brahmins, a thousand cows, a thousand poor innocent children, and a thousand weak and helpless women, shall be mine also. If I fail to act up to my vow, I shall be deemed a worse sinner than he that killed his own father and mother, than he that misappropriated the money set apart for the upkeep of a charity, than he that demolished a temple.' Thus spake this noble king of the lunar race, this martial Kshatriya.

"Thus resolved, this brave warrior who routed in battle even Indra at once set himself to his task, and courted the assistance of Krishna to secure for him the *Pasupathasthra*, that war instrument of Mahadeva which alone could kill Sindhava. Then said our saviour Krishna; and who is he but the *Avatar* of Vishnu—'Who am I?' he said. 'I am none other than Brahma, the creator. I am none other than Vishnu, the preserver, and I am Siva, the destroyer. I am all three in onc. I am one in three. Did I not teach you this great truth before you went to battle against the Kurus—that in whatever place, at whatever time, in whatever manner, and in whatever form, my believers wish to worship me, I will, in that place, at that time, in that manner, and in that very form, appear before them and grant their prayer. I am the one great power in the universe, the great cause which is itself without a cause. And what are Brahma, Vishnu, and Siva, but the attributes of one great principle pervading the whole of the vast universe. All things in the world, men, beasts, birds, reptiles, all inanimate things, and even this vast universe, pass through three stages. They have their birth, their growth, and their decay; and of these three stages I am the cause. Hence I am called Brahma, the creator, Vishnu, the preserver, and Siva, the destroyer. Though I am called by these three names on account of the functions that I perform, still I am the one great principle in this universe that underlies all these, the uncaused, indestructible, ever-living principle. Worship me, therefore, in this very place, as Mahadeva, and you will have your prayer granted at once.' Accordingly Arjuna fell down and worshipped Krishna, and the *Pasupathasthra* of Siva was vouchsafed to him. Next morning, Arjuna rose, put on his best armour, and amidst the praises of bards who proclaimed his titles, the great deeds he achieved and his prowess and skill in war, amidst the beating of drums and the blessings of good and righteous men, went forth to the field of battle, resolved before the setting of the sun to slay Sindhava and give his carcase to the jackals and other beasts of the earth, and to the birds of the air, or die on the burning pyre true to the vow he so angrily uttered the previous night.

"What at this time was the state of matters in the enemy's camp? News of Arjuna's vow against Sindhava was carried to king Duriyodhana and his men, and sent a thrill of horror throughout the whole camp. The king and the commander-in-chief, the brave Drona, at once devised plans to save poor Sindhava from Arjuna's arrows. They said: 'This Sindhava is a brave man and we cannot afford to lose him. He is of immense service to us, and if till to-morrow night we manage to keep him out of Arjuna's reach, Sindhava will be saved, and Arjuna, true to his vow, will die himself on the burning pyre. Without Arjuna, the Pandava army is worth nothing, and could be very easily routed.' So saying, they made arrangements for keeping Sindhava out of the brave Arjuna's reach. Early in the morning, long before that warrior commenced to fight against them, they arranged their army in the forefront like a chariot; behind the chariot another portion of their large army was arranged in the form of a fish; and behind this fish formation a portion was arranged in the form of a lotus; and in the midst of this lotus formation, Sindhava, the object of brave Arjuna's search, was safely hidden. These formations were several miles in length. Drona, the commander-in-chief, placed himself in the forefront at the head of the army. Eighteen *akronis* of troops were engaged that day against Arjuna. You may perhaps ask how much an *akroni* is. This I will now tell you. One war chariot, one elephant, three horses, and five fighting men make one *panthi.* Three *panthis* make one *senimuka.* Three *senimukas* form one *gulma.* Three *gulmas* go to make one *gana.* Three *ganas* form one *vahini.* Three *vahinis* make one *prithana.* Three *prithanas* go to form one *chamu.* Three *chamus* make one *anikini*, and ten *anikinis* make one *akroni.* So that we have for each *akroni* 21,870 war chariots, 21,870 elephants, 65,610 horses, and 109,350 soldiers. And when I say that eighteen *akronis* of troops were engaged that day, you can realize for yourselves the magnitude of the army that opposed Arjuna.

"Nothing daunted, Arjuna went forth to battle and fought bravely. His wonderful exploits struck terror into the enemy's forces. But alas, it was midday when he with difficulty pierced into the midst of the chariot formation. He had still to break through the fish formation and the lotus formation behind it. He tried hard, but it was impossible for him to reach the place where Sindhava was hidden. It was beyond human power to accomplish this difficult task. The far-seeing Krishna noticed the gravity of the situation. The day was fast drawing to a close and the setting sun was gradually approaching the western horizon; and Arjuna was only able to get into the midst of the chariot formation. In these circumstances, Sindhava's death was an utter impossibility. Accordingly, when there were yet five *naligais*[1] ere the day should close, Krishna directed his *chakra* to hide the sun. The *chakra* did so, and darkness spread over the land. But how was it that the *chakra*, which is brighter than the sun, brought on darkness? This is the reason. Once upon a time, when the good king Ambarisha ruled the land, he wished to acquire religious merit by fasting on every *ekadasi* day, and taking his food with as many Brahmins as he could secure on the morning of the next day. In this matter, he acted strictly in accordance with the rules laid down in our *Shastras*. Indra grew envious of the good work which the king was doing, and requested the well-known *Rishi* Thuruvasaka

[1] A *naligai* is equivalent to twenty-four minutes.

to throw obstacles in the way of the king while engaged in the accomplishment of his vow. One morning, the *Rishi* went to the king in the disguise of a Brahmin and asked to be fed with the other Brahmins. The king consented, and requested Thuruvasaka to go to the river, and return as soon as possible after performing his morning ablutions. The Brahmin did not return, and king Ambarisha was in a dilemma. He did not know what to do. If he did not take his food early in the morning as enjoined in the holy writings, all the religious merit he had hitherto acquired by the strict performance of his vow would be lost; and if on the other hand he partook of his meals without the Brahmin who went to bathe, promising to return in time, he would be committing a great sin, for it is a great sin to eat food when a Brahmin is starving. While in this serious difficulty, he was advised to take a leaf of the sacred *Tulsi* plant and a little water. As soon as these were taken, the Brahmin returned, and seeing what the king had done, pronounced a curse upon him. Vishnu's *chakra*, which was guarding the king from all kinds of evils, was enraged at the wily and dishonest conduct of the *Rishi*, and began to pursue him with the intention of killing him. The poor *Rishi* ran to Indra, then to Siva, and then to Vishnu himself for protection. He fell at the feet of Vishnu and implored his pardon. Vishnu thereupon directed the *chakra* not to molest him any further. The *Rishi*, after being thus harassed and pursued, was so much vexed with the *chakra* that he cursed it, by saying that its brightness should vanish and that it should become as dark as the darkest thing in the universe. But when the *chakra* requested Vishnu to save it from this curse, it was ordained that its brightness should vanish only once.

"It was therefore on the occasion to which we now refer that it became dark; and the moment it was directed by Krishna to hide the sun, everything became dark and night seemed to be fast approaching. The birds of the air began to make for their nests, and man and beast were returning to their resting place after the day's labour. And poor Arjuna, what could he do? He had no other alternative but to have the pyre prepared. The sinner Duriyodhana, seeing that the day had come to a close, and being convinced that Arjuna would act in accordance with his vow, hastened to the place where the pyre was prepared, with Sindhava, Drona, and the other generals of his army, to witness the much wished for sight. The pyre was lighted, and Arjuna prepared himself for the awful doom by going round it thrice. Just as he was about to leap into the burning flames, Krishna interrupted him and said: 'O Arjuna! it is not meet that you should, amidst the tears of your brothers and friends and your faithful men and amidst the joyful shouts of the enemy, madly put on end to your life, all for mere sentiment. How many in the world's history have under similar circumstances changed their purpose! Do not therefore madly put an end to your useful career.' Arjuna replied: 'I will not swerve one jot or tittle from what I have solemnly sworn to perform. I have not succeeded in killing Sindhava, and I will therefore die myself.' 'But here is Sindhava before you and within easy reach of you,' said Krishna. 'Why not now kill him and thus save yourself from this terrible death?' 'No,' said the noble Arjuna, 'the sun has gone down into the western ocean and night has come on, and I will not soil my hand or tarnish the glory of this my faithful *gandiba* by killing him now.' But what,' said Krishna, 'if the sun still shines in the western skies and the day has not yet come to a close?' 'I will then kill Sindhava,' said Arjuna. Our saviour Krishna now withdrew the *chakra* and lo! the setting sun was shining in all his glory at the distance of four fathoms from the western horizon. The bow was strung, and in a twinkle the *Pasupathasthra* of Siva flew like lightning and severed Sindhava's head from his body, amidst the shouts and exultations of all good and virtuous men. Glory be to Krishna, this saviour of mankind, who is ever ready to assist the good and to punish the wicked, this Dispenser of Justice who protected the good and noble Arjuna from his awful doom. Let us all therefore unite in praising our Creator."

So saying, the preacher knelt down before the picture. Camphor was lighted, and the whole audience rising *en masse* and exultingly shouting the words *Krishna*, *Govinda*, *Gopala*, &c., knelt down before the picture.

In this speech, strange medley as it is of oriental exaggeration and extraordinary incident, we find a wonderful parallel to the incident related in the Bible, wherein it is said that "the sun stood still and the moon stayed, until the people had avenged themselves upon their enemies." Whether the scientific critics of the West have given the true explanation of this passage, I shall not attempt to discuss, but with regard to the wonderful incidents related in Nalla Pillai's speech I need hardly state that the boasted "age of reason" has not yet arrived in Indian villages, the people of which implicitly believe in whatever is written in their sacred writings.[1]

[1] With reference to the last paragraph of this chapter, the following letter appeared in the next issue of the *Madras Christian College Magazine* :—

"SIR,—While I read with pleasure Part XI. of 'Life in an Indian Village,' it struck me regarding 'the wonderful parallel to the incident related in the Bible,' that Mr. T. Ramakrishna has no need to go to 'the scientific critics of the West' for 'the true explanation,' if he had only remembered what Dr. Miller taught him in 1871, when he like myself sat at the Doctor's feet to study the Scriptures. The explanation then given was that the passage in the Bible is purely figurative and poetical, and, if I mistake not, it is a quotation from some Hebrew poet. A similar explanation from Nalla Pillai's grandson would have not only *not* misled his hearers to imagine miracles where there were none, but probably enhanced the beauty of the passage. But, as my friend says, the 'age of reason' has not yet arrived in Indian villages; nor, I may add, in many better places besides.

"If, however, it is contended that the event in the *Mahabharata* is a true miracle, that it is so believed by Nalla Pillai's grandson, by Hindus generally, and by T. Ramakrishna to the bargain, then I fail to see any 'wonderful parallel to the incident related in the Bible,' which to a critical student is no miracle at all. A CLASSMATE.

"*Narsapur*, 20-3-89."

XII.

The village drama—The story of Harischandra—General remarks regarding the Indian stage.

It was at dusk one day in the merry month of May that Muthu Naick, the *taliyari* of Kélambakam, came to the house of a relative of mine in a neighbouring village, where I was spending my holidays. He had a cadjan leaf neatly rolled up which contained an invitation from Kothundarama Mudelly to my relative to attend a dramatic performance which was to take place in his village that night. We sent intimation to the headman expressing our willingness to attend the performance. After taking a hearty supper, I started with a number of friends about nine o'clock. Our way lay not along macadamized roads or over fine bridges, but through fields, shady groves, channels, and sometimes right through the beds of dried tanks. We had to walk about four miles before we reached Kélambakam. The moon was shining brightly over us, and I saw on my way the people of a whole village set out together to go to Kélambakam. Young men I saw hastening towards the place in groups, and singing songs by turns. I saw old men relating to women and children on the way the story which they were going to see represented on the stage that night, and discussing the relative merits of the actors. Never shall I forget the sight that impressed me so vividly on that occasion. It was a fine moonlight night, and hundreds of simple villagers of all sorts and conditions issued from shady groves, walked through fields and beds of dried tanks, crossed channels, and kept pouring into Kélambakam from all quarters in their best attire. When we were about a mile from the village we heard the noise of some thousands of people from about thirty or forty villages assembled in the plains of Kélambakam. As soon as we reached the place we saw some five or six thousand people squatting on the ground, and it was several minutes before we could be taken through the densely packed assembly and safely seated on mats in the open space in the middle. There was no raised stage, no enclosure for the actors; we simply saw five or six actors of whom one was a female. We also saw two washermen with torches in their hands. The players live in a neighbouring village, and this is the troupe whose services are called into requisition by the people of about thirty or forty villages in the neighbourhood of Kélambakam. The players have some reputation as actors, and their remuneration is fixed at one pagoda, or seven shillings per night. Any presents they get in the shape of money or clothes of course they take to themselves. The play commenced about ten o'clock. The well-known story of Harischandra was represented on the stage. The following is a short account of the story.

Once upon a time a number of pious Brahmin travellers went about visiting different places in India, bathing in the holy waters and worshipping at the different shrines. On their way they visited Ayodhia (Oudh) which was then ruled by a young prince named Harischandra. He was a most virtuous ruler, truthful and honest; and the moment he heard of the holy

Brahmins, the prince went to meet them and received them kindly. They, highly pleased with the hospitality of the good prince, and with the beneficence and justice of his administration of the country, told him that the ruler of Canouj had a daughter whose matchless beauty they could not describe in words, and that she alone was fit to be his wife. Harischandra, who was then unmarried, was fascinated by the very favourable account given to him of the princess, and requested the Brahmins to go to the ruler of Canouj on his behalf and bring about a marriage between himself and the beautiful princess. The Brahmins consented, went to Canouj, and delivered their message to the king, at the same time speaking very highly of the qualities and virtues of the ruler of Oudh. A day for the *Svayamvara*[1] was selected, and the king asked the travellers to bring Harischandra to Canouj on the appointed day. The different princes of India were also duly informed of the occasion, in order that Chandramithi, the beautiful daughter

[1] *Svayamvara* (literally, *self-choice*)—the election of a husband by a princess or a daughter of a Kshatriya at a public assembly of suitors for the purpose.—*Monier Williams.*

of the ruler of Canouj, might from among the princely suitors select one as her husband. On the appointed day all the kings as well as Harischandra arrived at the beautiful town of Cannamapuri (the capital of Canouj), the streets of which were decked with flowers and evergreens for the occasion. The Rajahs assembled in the durbar hall, and the beautiful Chandramithi in befitting attire arrived there with her maids. The maids then took her to each prince, giving out his name, the country he ruled, what he was famous for, and so on. When Chandramithi approached Harischandra, she was struck with his beauty and manly appearance, and having already heard a good deal about him, immediately selected him as her husband and threw the flower garland round his neck. Immediately in that great assembly an unknown voice was heard which said: "Harischandra! it is willed by God that you should be the husband of the beautiful Chandramithi." The marriage ceremonies were duly performed, and some time afterwards Harischandra left for Oudh with his bride. Soon they were blest with a child, and for some time lived happily together.

One day in the audience chamber of Indra, the king of the gods, when there were present thirty-three crores of gods and forty-eight thousand *rishis*, the question arose as to whether there could be found in the nether world at least one truthful and honest man. To this the *rishi* Vathistha answered that Harischandra the ruler of Oudh was truthful and honest, and that the like of him could nowhere else be found. The *rishi* Viswamitra objected, and said that Harischandra was not as Vathishta had described him. A hot discussion ensued, and it was decided that if Harischandra could be proved to be a liar, the *rishi* Vathishta should forego all the merit he had acquired by his religious austerity; and that if Harischandra proved to be a really truthful and honest person, the *rishi* Viswamitra should present the king with one half of the merit which he had acquired by the penance which he had performed.

Viswamitra then left the Indra Sabha and at once sent a few of his followers to the king to request him for some money toward the due performance of some religious rites. Harischandra willingly promised to pay whatever money was required. The money was ready, but Viswamitra entrusted it to the king, saying that he would take it on a future occasion. Soon after, the *rishi* sent two beautiful girls to the king, directing them to dance and sing before him. They went, and in the presence of the king vied with each other in exhibiting their skill in dancing and singing. The king was highly pleased, and asked if they had any request to make. They replied that they wished to marry him. The prince grew angry, and said that their request was an improper one. They however, persisted, and said that he must marry them. The king thereupon ordered his peons to remove the girls from his presence. The girls returned and informed Viswamitra of what had taken place, and the *rishi*, greatly enraged at the treatment which the girls received at the hands of the king, immediately went to him and asked him to marry the girls. The prince replied: "My lord! I will do anything for you, but I will not marry those girls." "You will do anything for me?" said Viswamitra. "Undoubtedly, my lord," replied the prince. "Then give me your riches, your country, and all that you possess," asked the *rishi*. The king at once gave these and also the jewels which he, his wife, and his son were then wearing, and so in a short time became a beggar. He requested the *rishi* to permit him to depart from his country. Permission was given and the king went away. The *rishi* suddenly called the king back and reminded him of the promise which he had made in regard to the sum of money required for the due performance of certain religious rites. Harischandra said: "My lord! you know my present position. You have taken away even my clothes, and I am now a beggar. However, if you insist upon my paying the money, I beg you will allow me forty days' time." Viswamitra consented to this, and accordingly sent with the prince one of his men to receive the money at the end of the forty days, taking care at the same time to advise his man to receive his wages from the king for remaining with him for forty days. Harischandra, with his wife, his son, and a few of his faithful followers, left Oudh amidst the tears of his people, and at the end of twenty days, after much toil and many difficulties reached Benares. There the king sold his wife and son to a Brahmin for the money due to Viswamitra, and executed to him what is called a *murisittu* (slavery agreement); and that he might be able to pay the wages due to Viswamitra's man, he went and sold himself to the pariah who kept watch over the burning-ground. Thenceforward Harischandra became the servant of the pariah and received for each corpse brought to the burning-ground half a fanam (one penny), one cubit (half a yard) of new cloth and a handful of rice. He gave the penny and the new cloth to his pariah master, and reserved to himself the handful of rice which he cooked with his own hands and ate.

Thus was the ruler of Oudh reduced to the position of a burning-ground watchman with a pariah for his master, and his queen to that of a servant woman in the house of a Brahmin. One day while things were in this condition, their only son went with some other youngsters of the town to the fields to fetch some *durba* grass. While the young man was plucking the grass in the fields, he was bitten by a cobra and fell down dead. The youngsters returned home and related the sad story to poor Chandramithi. She, in the midst of her sorrow for the death of her beloved boy, performed her daily work, and in the evening took leave of her mistress in order that she might go and burn her son's corpse. It was now getting dark; but she fearlessly went in search of the child, found the dead body, and took it to the burning-ground, with some fuel which she had collected with her own hands. Harischandra, who was watching the burning-ground, finding that some one was secretly disposing of a dead body, came near and asked the woman to give the usual penny, cloth, and rice. She said she was too poor to give these. Harischandra would not allow the corpse to be burnt. He said he would for her sake forego the handful of rice, but not the penny nor the cloth which should go to his master. He knew that it was the dead body of his son, and yet he was determined to serve his master honestly. Accordingly he insisted on his wife's paying the money and the cloth. The woman left the dead body and went away, promising to return with the money and the cloth from her master. The night was now far advanced.

It so happened that on that very night some robbers had entered the house of the Maharajah of Benares, and taken the child that was sleeping in the cradle, and after stripping it of all its valuable jewels, had killed it and thrown its dead body on the street. Chandramithi seeing the dead body, began to weep, for the child was like her own. Then came the king's servants in search of the child, and finding it in the hands of the woman, at once took her before the king, who, convinced that she had murdered his child, ordered Chandramithi to be beheaded. The executioner, who was none other than Harischandra's master, delegated that work to his servant, and he, regardless of the fact that the unfortunate victim was his own wife, tied her hands, and with his sword in his hand led her to the place of execution amid the tears of the people of Benares.

While Harischandra was thinking of his miserable condition, Viswamitra came on the scene and said: "O Harischandra, you have lost your dominions, your wealth, your dignity, and your only beloved son; and now with your own hand your are going to put an end to the life of your dear wife. Now, do but tell a lie and I will restore to you your lost dominions, your riches, and your former dignity. I will bring your son to life and restore him to you, and I will also see your wife's innocence declared." The king bravely replied: "My lord! it is written that to kill a thousand cows is as sinful as to kill one child; to kill a thousand children is as sinful as taking the life of a weak and helpless woman; and to kill a thousand women is as heinous as the crime of slaying a Brahmin; but to tell a lie is worse than killing a thousand Brahmins. Do you wish me, my lord, to commit such a great sin? I have lost my country, my wealth, my dignity, my only beloved son, and now with my own hand I am about to put an end to the life of my dear wife, all for the sake of truth. I will not tell a lie, even at the risk of my own life." The *rishi* Viswamitra went away ashamed. The king now thought of his miserable condition and shed tears at the thought of losing his wife. The brave Chandramithi encouraged him and said: "Do not, my dear husband, be afraid to slay me. The cause of truth and virtue is more valuable that my life. Do not delay, but slay me at once." Then Harischandra, in firm tones and with his sword in his hand, said to his wife: "If it is true that there is one God, if it is true that throughout my whole career in this world I have walked in the path of truth and virtue, and if it is true also that this my wife is chaste and virtuous, then let my wife's head be severed from her body at one stroke." So saying he drew his sword, and immediately there was seen a garland of flowers on the neck of the beautiful Chandramithi. Indra and all the *rishis*, Brahma, Vishnu, and Siva came there, praised the king for his truth, showered their blessings on him, restored him to his former position, and brought back to life his dead son and the child of the ruler of Benares. The king with his wife and son returned to Oudh and ruled the country for many years.

The story of Harischandra which I have thus related is the most popular story in India, and is written in almost all the languages of the country. The name Harischandra is synonymous with truth and virtue.

I should state that the whole of the story was not acted on the occasion on which I was present. It was divided into six parts, the last of which was performed on that occasion. As I have already stated, there were present some thousands of people, so that the crowd covered three or four acres of ground on which the people squatted. There was no charge for seeing the performance. The richest land-holder, the high-caste Brahmin and the meanest pariah were there. The respectable portion of the audience was seated near the actors. There was no enclosure, no stage; there were no screens; a white cloth served this purpose. The play commenced about ten o'clock. The white cloth was removed and the characters appeared on the scene, with painted faces and gaudy jewels and dresses. A little of the story was acted, and then a great many things unconnected with the play were witnessed. Witty remarks were made, and songs were sung. The buffoon now and then related amusing stories. The granting of rewards also formed part of the programme. Every respect-able villager called the buffoon and placed some money in his hands. The buffoon immediately repaired to his place, and called out in a loud voice the name of the person who gave the reward, his village and all concerning him, and in conclusion said that a rich reward was given. The reward in many cases was no more than two annas (threepence). This went on for some time, and then part of the play was given. Stories unconnected with the play were again related, songs were again sung, and presents were again given, many of them being old clothes. In this way things went on till six in the morning, by which time the play was ended and the people had dispersed to their homes.

From what I have said it will be seen that the arrangements made by the villagers whenever they get up a theatrical performance are very simple and cost little or no money; but the sense of enjoyment is none the less keen. Throughout the whole proceedings I carefully noted how the simple villagers appreciated the play. They seemed to enter thoroughly into the spirit of the story, and I heard one of them use very strong language with regard to the *rishi* Viswamitra. I saw women shedding tears and saying: "Viswamitra is a Chandala. He is a sinner. No doubt he will be punished for his mean actions and sent to the worst part of hell." One woman was actually heard to exclaim: "Is there no God above to punish the wretch Viswamitra? Is there no lightning to descend at once and kill him on the spot?

Will not mother earth open at once and devour his detested body?"

Indian actors are not much respected in society. Their remuneration is small—so small that a whole troupe may receive no more than seven shillings a night, and altogether the profession is considered a low one in this country.

XIII.

Feasts and festivals—The Pongal feast—Description of a festival in the temple—The story of the queen who committed suttee.

One morning in January there was an unusual stir in the village of Kélambakam. The *Pongal*, the national feast of the Hindus, was to be celebrated on that day. For some days before, the inhabitants of the village, both male and female, were busy making preparations for the coming feast. Damages caused to houses during the recent rainy season were duly repaired, and the women were engaged up to the previous day in plastering the mud walls and the men in harvesting a portion of their crops, getting the grain husked, and making everything ready for the important feast. New faces were seen at the time in the village. Young men who had married girls from Kélambakam arrived in time to enjoy the feast in the houses of their fathers-in-law. On the morning of the feast day, the women were up betimes and were busily engaged at all sorts of work. Some were seen cleaning the floor with cow-dung solution and drawing quaint figures with powdered chalk; some dusting the roofs of houses and cleaning old pots, and others decking door-posts with saffron and the red powder called *kunkumam* and putting strings of mango leaves over the doorways. Little girls were seen in the streets arranging in various forms lumps of cowdung and covering them with pumpkin flowers. The potter was the busiest man in the whole village; and pots of various shapes and sizes were carried from his house by the women. Presents of vegetables were exchanged between the people of Kélambakam and those of the neighbouring villages. The *purohita* Ramanuja Charriar rose earlier than usual, and after finishing his morning ablutions went forth and visited every household, informing the inmates as to the most propitious time when the pots should be placed on the fire, &c., and the people listened with eagerness to every one of his sayings. The whole village assumed a gay appearance. There was a cessation of work, and feasting and merriment were to be found everywhere.

According to Hindu notions the year is divided into two equal portions. The first half commences in January, and the second half, which commences in July, lasts till December. The latter is said to belong to the *Asuras* (evil spirits), and is therefore considered to be a very bad time for man. Everything is gloomy then, and people do not think of pleasure. Then come most of their trials and difficulties, for during the rainy season they must think of nothing but their fields and their cultivation. The other portion of the year is considered to belong to the *Dévas* (gods); and then festivities take place and there is merriment everywhere, At this time of the year, marriages are performed and festivals celebrated in temples in honour of Hindu deities. The *Pongal* feast is celebrated on the first day of this joyful portion of the year, which falls about the second week in January. The idea is, that, before the grain that is harvested is used for human consumption, a portion should be converted into rice, cooked, and offered to the Sun and Indra.

Indra is the god of rain, and the people are enjoined to worship him on this day and thus show their gratitude to him for having vouchsafed rain at the proper seasons. This has been the practice from time immemorial, though once upon a time Krishna, when he was spending his boyhood with the shepherds of Ayarpadi, asked them not to worship Indra, but to offer their devotions to the cows which supplied them with milk, &c., and to the hills whereon the cows grazed. "Indra," he said, "sends rain for the benefit of those who cultivate the fields. The rain is of no use to us. We live by our cattle, and it is meet therefore that we should on this important occasion give our rice-offerings to the cows that supply us with milk and to the hills which supply them with grass and the various kinds of herbs upon which they feed." To this the shepherds consented, and accordingly they went to the hill called Góvarthanagiri and there worshipped their cattle as directed by Krishna. Indra, seeing that the homage paid to him by the people from time immemorial had been withdrawn, grew envious, and directed the clouds to send down rain. For some days it rained very heavily, with the result that the country around was flooded and all the people suffered except the shepherds, who were saved by Krishna. The shepherds, as soon as they saw that Indra was determined to punish them by sending rain, flocked to Krishna and requested him to save them from the anger of Indra. Krishna thereupon lifted the hill of Góvarthana with one finger and held it over his people like an umbrella. The shepherds were saved, but the people of the country round about suffered much on account of the heavy rains. They all ran to Indra and said : "Save us from thy fury, O Indra! the rain is pouring and is causing immense destruction to our property. The shepherds who broke off their allegiance to you are safe under the protection of Krishna, while we, who remain faithful to you, are the real sufferers." Indra saw the false step he had taken, and immediately stopped the rain; then seeing that Krishna, the Avatar of Vishnu, took the shepherds under his protection, went and stood penitent before him. Then said Krishna: "Indra! I did not wish to trench upon your rights. I only wanted to punish you for your pride and teach you a lesson. I am satisfied that you are now humbled, and henceforth the people of the world shall continue to worship you on the first day as has hitherto been done, but, in commemoration of this event they shall on the following day cook rice and offer it to their cattle." Such is the origin of the second day's *pongal* called the *cattle pongal.* (The word *pongal* means boiling.)

Accordingly, on this day, in the open space inside every house in Kélambakam, a number of huge pots, three or five as the case might be, were placed on the fire in a line, at the time directed by the *purohita*, Ramanuja Charriar. The new pots were all well cleaned and smeared over with saffron. White and red marks were also put on. A quantity of rice with as much water as it would absorb in the cooking was put into each pot, and some milk was also poured in. The boiling of the rice was anxiously watched, and when it began to simmer the youngsters of each house shouted several times the word *pongal.* The shouting took place at about the same time in every dwelling in the village, from which it may be inferred that all the people without exception acted strictly in accordance with the directions given to them by their venerable *purohita* regarding the auspicious time for placing the rice pots on the fire. When the rice was boiled, the pots were very carefully lifted out and placed in safe positions. A handful of the cooked rice was then taken from each pot, and after being mixed with ghee, sugar, and fruits, was offered to the sun. Coconuts were then broken and camphor was lighted. Then all the members of the family knelt down before the sun and worshipped him. After this the males sat down for meals in two rows in the *kutam* or hall of the house. Plantain leaves were first spread out, and a number of vegetable preparations were served. These were placed near the edges of the leaves rice being served in the centre. The place of honour in the dining-hall was given to the son-in-law. A little of the rice served was first mixed with *dhal* and ghee, and eaten. Then a little was taken with some vegetable broth. After this came the third course, when the remaining rice was taken with pepper water. A fresh helping of rice was then given, which was eaten with butter-milk. Between the third and fourth courses, cakes and sweet drinks were served. Thus ended the midday meal of the first day of the *Pongal,* to the villagers a most sumptuous feast. The males then took betel and nut and, smearing their bodies with sandal, retired to rest. After this the females sat down for meals. Lastly the servants were fed in their masters' houses.

On the morning of the second day, the *cattle pongal* feast was celebrated. As on the previous day, although not on so large a scale, rice was cooked, but on this day it was given to the cows. The cattle were not sent out of the village to graze. They were all taken to the tank and well washed. Their horns were painted and garlands of flowers and foliage were thrown round their necks, and they were led in procession through the streets of the village with tom-toms and music. Then commenced a round of festivities. The people went about visiting each other. It is said that when Indra punished the people by sending heavy rain, they were not able to stir out. They were shut up in their houses for some days, and then when the rain ceased they ran about in all directions, anxiously inquiring of friends and relatives how they had survived the destructive rain ; and it was in commemoration of this event that the villagers went about inquiring after the welfare of each other. The first question asked when two persons met was: "Has the milk boiled?" Then some complimentary questions were exchanged, and in token of the goodwill existing between them, betel and nut were offered. These mutual visits lasted for some days. The pariahs and the menial servants of the village also made merry at this season. Some disguised themselves as *byragees* (wandering mendicants from the north), others as *pandarams* (professional beggars who sing religious songs). Their powers of imitation were much applauded by the villagers, who gave them presents. The dancing girls of the temple also visited all the houses in the village, along with a number of musicians, and after dancing and singing for some time received presents. The young girls of the parcherry, about ten or twelve in number, led by an elderly lady, went about singing songs. The girls formed a ring round a certain object, and went round it several times singing songs and clapping their hands. New cloths were bought and worn for the first time on this important occasion. The sons-in-law who came to the village to enjoy the feast had valuable cloths given to them, as also had their wives. On receiving their presents they fell at the feet of their fathers-in-law and mothers-in-law as a token of gratitude and respect. The youngsters also prostrated themselves at the feet of their elders and received their blessings.

Amidst all these rejoicings the temple deity was not forgotten. One day was set apart for celebrating a festival in the temple. Early in the morning, about five o'clock, several rockets were sent up, by means of which the villagers were apprised of the festival in the temple. The people, as soon as they heard the sound of the rockets, arose, and after bathing and putting on the usual marks, got ready coconuts, fruits, flowers, and camphor. The idol of the temple was placed on a vehicle and was carried through the streets of the village. It stopped at every house, and the inmates taking the coconuts, fruits, flowers, and camphor, came out and worshipped the god. At about eight oclock, the idol was taken to the top of a neighbouring hill on which there is a very ancient *mandapam* (porch) built of granite stones. The hill, which is at a distance of about two miles from Kélambakam and which slopes up from the banks of the river Palar, is about five hundred feet in height. There is a fine flight of steps, ten or twelve feet broad, leading to the porch at the top. The hill is called *Ammamalai*, *i.e.*, literally, the mother's hill. The following is the explanation given of the origin of the name. The story goes that in old days this part of the country was ruled by a petty prince. He had a very beautiful wife and a young daughter. On one occasion he had to leave his home to fight for his country. He was absent for several years and his queen, a very brave woman, ruled the country wisely and well during her husband's absence. After the lapse of a few years, the prince returned, and burning with the desire to see his beloved queen after such a long separation ran to the fort at the top of the hill. There he saw a woman, a girl of sixteen summers, coming out of a tank after her morning bath, the water still dripping from her cloth and her long flowing hair. In her the prince saw the likeness of his own dear wife, and soon ran to embrace her. The beautiful maiden was struck with terror, and, seeing a stranger approaching, sprang into the water; but before doing so, cursed the man. The maiden was drowned and was seen no more; and the king fell down dead as soon as the curse was pronounced. The bold queen, seeing the fate of her beloved husband and her beautiful daughter, had a pyre prepared, and between the dead bodies of both laid herself down to die. The fire was lighted and all three were consumed to ashes. Just over the spot where they were burnt the *mandapam* was built by a loving people. The fort is now no more, nor does the tank exist in which was drowned the fair girl whose career of brilliant promise was cut short by a father's unfortunate mistake and unbridled passion. But their sites are still pointed out by the people. Such is the local tradition. Every tree, every rock, in fact every spot has its tradition, and even to this day unmarried girls hold in veneration the unhappy virgin and pray to her to bless them with good husbands; and married women, in order that they may enjoy the married state till death, worship her,

> "who counted it
> A sin her noble husband to survive,
> And in a moment flung her life away."

To the top of this hill and to this porch connected with so many sad associations the god was taken, and there during the day it was bathed in rose water, milk, curd, &c. In the evening, the idol was placed on a vehicle profusely decked with flowers and jewels. The sight on the top of the hill was really grand. Thousands of people were seen below eagerly waiting to catch a glimpse of their god as he issued from the porch. The course of the river Palar was clearly visible for miles, and all round were smiling fields and nestling villages. Nor was the spectacle from below, when the idol had been brought down from the top, less imposing. The light of numberless torches and blue flames blended with that of the setting sun and the rising moon, and falling upon the Brahmins who recited the sacred Vedas and upon thousands of simple villagers in their holiday dress, densely packed all along the flight of steps from the top of the hill to the bottom, gave a beauty and charm to the scene that to be realized must be actually witnessed. Such a scene would form a fit theme for a poet or a painter. In the midst of this immense crowd were seen sellers of toys, professional bards reciting interesting stories, jugglers and acrobats exhibiting their feats, beggars with torches in their hands, and last, but not least, the members of a religious association all dressed alike and singing songs in praise of their deity. An account of this religious association I must reserve for another paper.

XIV.

The religious brotherhood—How they followed the temple idol and sang sacred lyrics.

In my last paper, I referred to a religious association, the members of which followed the temple idol, when it was carried in procession, and sang sacred lyrics. In a neatly built room, in the middle of the village, surrounded on all sides by a flower garden, is the meeting place of this religious association, which in Tamil is called *Bajanakutam*. At the entrance over the gateway is represented the trident mark of the Vishnava sect with the figures of Garuda and Hanuman on either side. Inside, on the walls all round, are hung pictures representing the different incarnations of Vishnu, and on the floor are seen scattered in confusion various musical instruments. Here in this room, consecrated to Vishnu, the members of the *Bajana-*

kutam meet for worship. The day on which the festival described in my last paper took place, was a gala day with the people of the association. All the members were present on the occasion, and followed the idol to the top of the hill, and in the evening when it was taken down in procession they displayed unusual interest in their work and did their utmost to please the people. They were all dressed alike, with sandal abundantly smeared over their bodies. Their hind-locks were profusely decked with flowers. The chief man of the association, who is also the most intelligent, had what is called a *tambour* resting on his right shoulder, and he dexterously passed his forefinger over the steel wires of the instrument, while in his left hand he had two small pieces of wood with iron rings and small bells attached. The sound produced by striking the two pieces of wood against each other, blending with the tinkling of the small bells, produced a curious effect. This musician had, besides, strings of small bells tied round his legs. Thus accoutred, he sang in a loud voice and also danced, with both his hands engaged. Another member of the *Bajanakutam* played the drum, while a third played the fiddle. Two or three had small circular shaped metallic instruments which when struck against each other sent forth sharp shrill sounds. To the accompaniment of these musical instruments the members of the association sang sacred songs when following the idol. There were hundreds of people near the singing party who seemed to thoroughly enter into the spirit of what was sung. Their faces beamed with joy, and some actually danced and clapped their hands. It may interest my readers to have translations of one or two of the songs sung on the occasion to which I refer. Here is one :—

> Trust firmly in one God and thus be saved, O mind!
> Do not be born again by trusting in false gods,
> It is not easy for the lame, O mind!
> To reach the honeycomb upon the tree
> And drink of its sweet honey. Even so
> 'Tis hard for sinful men to contemplate
> The sacred name of Govinda, O mind!
>
> Trust firmly in one God and thus be saved, O mind!
> Do not be born again by trusting in false gods.
> Thou know'st how powerless is the frog to cull
> Sweet nectar from the lotus. Even so
> To sinful men no happiness affords
> The sweet and sacred name of Bagavan.

Trust firmly in one God and thus be saved, O mind!
Do not be born again by trusting in false gods.
Say if the ass, that carries on his back
The *kung'ma* flower,[1] its uses understands:
E'en so, are fools and madmen helpless to
Discern the greatness of our Venkatésa.

Trust firmly in one God and thus be saved, O mind!
Do not be born again by trusting in false gods.
'Tis only Siva who can understand
The goodness in the sacred name of God.
E'en so, the virtuous and the good alone
Are able to discern the highest truths.

Trust firmly in one God and thus be saved, O mind!
Do not be born again by trusting in false gods.
Know well what has been taught to thee, O mind!
By the great Thathadésikar, and thus
Enjoy the presence of Parankusa
Who lives in heaven, the dwelling-place of God.

Here is another :—

Be saved by meditating every day
On Ramanama *mantra*, thou, O mind!

It is the only *mantra* that to us
Affords salvation sure from all our sins.

It is the sacred *mantra*, thou, O mind!
That saved Gajanthra in the hour of need.

It is the *mantra*, thou, O mind! that gave
The never ending cloth to Draupatha.

[1] A costly flower used in Indian medicines.

It is the sacred *mantra*, thou, O mind!
That Prakalath to mankind so well taught.

It is the sacred *mantra*, thou, O mind!
That with Govarthana the shepherds saved.

It is the sacred *mantra*, thou, O mind!
That to Valmiki showed the way to heaven.

It is the sacred *mantra*, thou, O mind!
That to his wife great Siva taught of old.

It is the *mantra*, thou, O mind! that saved
Kabir and Ramdoss in this *kaliyug*.

It is the *mantra*, thou, O mind! that gives
Eternal joy to good and virtuous men.

It is the sacred *mantra*, thou, O mind!
That to Parankusa gave joy divine.

Such are specimens of the lyrics sung by the members of the *Bajanakutam*. It may be well that I should explain briefly the various allusions in the latter. The third stanza refers to the story of Gajanthra having once gone to drink water in a channel and been caught by a crocodile. For several days the elephant had neither food nor water, and his life was in imminent danger. At last when he had no strength to extricate himself from his perilous position and was about to be dragged into the water, he thought of Vishnu. It is said that Vishnu immediately appeared and saved him.

The allusion in the next stanza is to the story which appears in the *Mahabaratha*, one of the two great national epics of the Hindus. Duriyodhana of the Kurus wanted to insult the chaste Draupatha, of the Pandus, before a large assembly, and with this object he directed that she should be stripped of her cloth. Draupatha thought of Vishnu, and thereupon the cloth which she was wearing went on increasing in length. The result was that the person charged with the duty of stripping grew tired, and Draupatha was saved.

The next stanza refers to one of the most popular stories in India. Prakalath was the son of Hirania, who tried to dissuade him from owning Vishnu as his god by punishing him in various ways. But Prakalath would not renounce Vishnu, and in the end was saved, while Hirania was killed by Vishnu himself.

The story of Krishna lifting the hill of Govarthanagiri to save the shepherds will be found fully related in my last chapter.

It is said that Valmiki, the renowned author of the *Ramayana*, was at first an illiterate hunter, but that by having been taught constantly to utter the word *Rama* he came to understand the divine truths, and afterwards by inspiration wrote the grand epic.

It is said that Siva once taught his wife about the greatness of Vishnu. It is believed that Kabir, a Muhammadan, and Rama Doss, a Hindu, were in very recent times (in the present *kaliyuga*) saved by Vishnu for believing in him even at the risk of their lives.

The above stories are known to the most ignorant villager, so that the references to them in the pieces sung by the members of the *Bajanakutam* were highly appreciated. Also the references made in the first piece to the ass that bears the *kunguma* flower, the lame man that wishes to reach the honeycomb on the tree, and the frog that is unable to extract the honey from the lotus, are so well known that every one understands them. In fact, there are proverbial sayings founded on them which every Hindu is able to quote. Further, the language in which the above lyrics and all similar lyrics are expressed is very plain and simple. Although they are written with full regard for the rules of Tamil prosody, they are nevertheless easily understood, as they are intended for the masses. There is still another peculiar characteristic to be found in these pieces, and that is the reference made to Siva, who, it is said, has acknowledged the superiority of Vishnu. The Saivites do not admit this, and the Saivites and Vishnuvites hate each other most intensely.

The members of the *Bajanakutam* honour and respect one another greatly. When two members meet, they fall at each other's feet and exchange kind words. At these times they use a language peculiar to themselves, and which is called in Tamil *Paribasha*. In this article and the previous one I have given a brief account of the great feast of *Pongal*, which to Hindus is as important as Christmas is to Christians, and of the religious association existing in Kélambakam, the members of which follow the village idol and sing sacred lyrics.

XV.

Concluding Remarks.

I have thus far tried to present my readers with a picture of life in an Indian village. There are a good many more subjects connected with it upon which a great deal could be written. Much might be said about the sports and games daily indulged in by the village people, as well as about marriage and funeral ceremonies, which, however, are not peculiar to villages only. Reference might also be made to the village *panchayets*, of which most of my readers have probably heard. In former times disputes regarding property and caste differences, and disputes arising from breaches of social morality, were all decided by the *panchayets*, a tribunal composed of five of the most respectable members of the village.

A description of this old and useful institution, which is fast dying out, would be out of place in what professes to be an account of village life as it is at the present day. I hope I have made my sketches of village life in Southern India sufficiently complete to induce in my readers an interest in the welfare of the toiling people who form the majority in this, the greatest dependency of the British Empire. Before closing, however, I wish to make a few reflections on what appears to me noticeable features of Indian village life.

The first is the extreme importance attached to religion. Every other thing gives way to this important aspect of Hindu life. In religion, the Hindu lives, moves, and has his being. His whole action, his whole thought, all that he does day by day, and on occasions of marriages and funeral ceremonies, is tinged with religion. The one pervading idea with the Hindu is how to get rid of future births and obtain eternal beatitude. We have seen how in dramatic performances gods are introduced to bless a truthful and honest man, how educated animals are trained to act the parts of Rama, Lakshmana, and Sita, and how in popular tales recited in Hindu homes the religious element is largely introduced. We thus find religion to be the foundation of everything Hindu. The very construction of an Indian village bears ample evidence to this fact. A temple is built and dedicated to the deity worshipped, and round the temple a village springs up. It is a rare phenomenon in India, at least in Southern India, to find a village without a temple. The religious Hindu will not settle down in a village where there is no temple, and where, accordingly, he has no chance of acquiring religious merit. Our ancient rajahs were careful, when establishing a new village, to build a temple in the centre and endow it munificently. There is also to be found in every Indian village a small temple built in honour of the *gramathevatha* (village deity), which is said to guard the village from all sorts of pestilential diseases. I have given a description of Angalammal, the deity of Kélambakam, and the doings of the temple priest, from which my readers will have learned how the lower classes of the people frequent the temple, carrying flesh, liquor, and other things with them. This custom among Hindus, of worshipping gods and goddesses supposed to preside over pestilential diseases and evil spirits, seems to be a remnant of pre-Aryan times, which on account of the cowardice of the Hindu and his natural delicacy of feeling concerning religion has continued down to the present day. This is the reason why we find this base form of religion prevailing amongst the lower classes of the people, even after the introduction of the purer and higher religion of the Brahmins.

We have seen, however, that the constitution of a village makes provision for the higher religion. We have seen how grants of land have been made for the due performance of worship in the temples. The temple priests and the Brahmin *Purohita*, who minister to the religious wants of the villagers, have also lands set apart for their use. The lands given to these men are larger in extent than those given to the other servants of the village community; thus showing that religion is deemed of the highest importance by the villagers.

A second important feature of village life is the desire on the part of the inhabitants to secure facilities for water. The village of Kélambakam is situated, as we have seen, on the borders of the river Palar, and it will be found that the large towns and villages in India are generally built on the banks of rivers, or wherever there is plenty of water obtainable. There is also in Kélambakam a large tank, and all villages which are not irrigated by rivers and channels have tanks large enough to hold water to irrigate the fields for about six months in the year. There are also to be found in villages tanks of smaller dimensions, neatly built by the side of the temple, to which the villagers, both male and female, go every morning to bathe. Water is of the utmost importance to the Hindu villager, and really forms one of the inducements for him to settle down in a village. In tropical climates, and in a country like India, where agriculture forms the chief occupation of the people, water is highly necessary. It is also very necessary for the daily ceremonies of the Hindus. Daily washing is enjoined as a religious duty. No wonder, therefore, that we find Hindus sacrificing everything else for water convenience. When two Hindus meet and make inquiries of each other's welfare, the first question asked is whether their respective villages have been blest with rain. Again, when two strangers meet and speak about the relative merits of their villages, the palm is given to the village that can boast of what is called *jalasavukiam* (water convenience). It is in watering places that we find people, male and female, meeting and talking all sorts of scandals. It is there that one gets all the news of the village. The construction of a Hindu village depends largely on the water facilities which the selected site affords.

The third thing that strikes me as noticeable is the mutual service system, which is here carried to perfection and practised with success. We in modern times are accustomed to use money as the medium by which we obtain all our requirements. But in Indian villages from time immemorial it has been the practice to render mutual service. The barber attends to the carpenter in return for service rendered to him in making ploughs and other necessary wooden implements. In return for the crow-bar, sickle, and spade supplied by the black-smith, the potter makes cooking vessels and pots for storing grain and other articles of human consumption. The washerman washes the clothes of the *vythian* (physician). This system does not promote competition among village workmen, and the result is that village artisans have not reached a very high state of efficiency in their work. This is one of the disadvantages of the system of mutual service, and there are others, but it has on the whole very well suited the conditions and circumstances of India.

Still another thing that strikes me as interesting is that each village is a little state in itself, with its king in the person of the headman, its minister of finance in the person of the karnam, and so on. There is unity and perfection even in small things, and the meanest villager is thus educated in the art of government, for what is a Hindu kingdom but a congeries of small kingdoms modelled exactly on the principles that govern the larger kingdom?

The chief characteristics of Indian villagers are their simplicity, contentment, and habits of working hard. In food, in dress, and in many other things they are simple. They are not silly and do not waste money on mere frivolities. Although it is true that Hindus show a lamentable weakness for jewels, the charge cannot be laid at the door of the villagers. They are very contented, and they have no high ambitions. If they get enough of rain, and are able to raise sufficient food to sustain them for a year, they are satisfied. They work very hard, and do not think of anything else but their work. They work when there is work, and play when there is no work, and enjoy life's pleasures most keenly. If in England public recitations are given by men who have studied the art of elocution to perfection, the simple villager of India has his bards to recite to him interesting old tales for a handful of rice. If civilized Europe can boast of highly trained horses and other intelligent animals, acrobats performing extraordinary gymnastic feats, and jugglers doing wonderful things, the Indian villager has his jugglers and acrobats, his snake-charmers and animal-tamers, ready to show their skill for a small sum. If in other countries opera-houses, theatres, and other similar public places of amusement are maintained at enormous cost, the poor Indian rustic has his village troupe to amuse him for seven shillings a night. And if in foreign countries learned divines thrill the hearts of their congregations with the fire of their eloquence, the villagers here have their preacher to sermonize on the popular incidents of the *Ramayana* and the *Mahabaratha.* But there is an important difference between the two. In the one the highly trained and civilized mind of Europe yearns after perfection in social delights and enjoyments, and cares not how much money is spent, while the Indian villager rests satisfied with what was instituted for his amusement hundreds of years ago, and which time and the altered circumstances of the country have not in the least changed.

A very marked characteristic of the Indian villager is his extremely conservative nature. His life in general flows smoothly on, unruffled by anything uncommom, and undisturbed by the many conflicting interests that are at work in the outside world. Of these he has scarcely an idea. Centuries of isolation have confined him to his home, and even in modern times the civilizing agencies that are at work elsewhere leave him unaffected. To quote the words of Professor Max Müller: "The village is his world, and the sphere of public opinion with its beneficial influences seldom extends beyond the horizon of his village." A stereotyped and a highly conservative mode of living is adopted which often leads him to look down with contempt upon the changes which are being wrought every day around him, and everything with him seems, as Carlyle would say, "to lie at anchor in the stream of time regardless of all changes." Years have rolled away, changes have been vast and varied, and changes of government have been many, and still the Indian villager resembles exactly his prototype of at least one thousand years ago.

But even this extreme conservatism of the Indian villager has to contend against the highly progressive tendencies of modern times. "The ways of the world," to quote Carlyle once more, "are more anarchical than ever. . . . We have got into the age of revolutions. All kinds of things are coming to be subjected to fire as it were; hotter and hotter the wind rises around everything." India is now advancing at a remarkably rapid rate, and new features are appearing even in the life of an Indian village. It is not my intention here to enumerate all those new features that have arisen, but I will mention two which seem to me to be very important, and which will require to be looked into sooner or later.

Owing to the nature of land taxation in India, by which payment of revenue is made in coin and not in grain, as was the case in olden times during the days of Hindu rajahs, a new class of people have sprung up who of all the people seem to be particularly favoured in their trade. These are the money-lenders, and every village has its usurer. I have in my account of Muthusamy Chetty, the usurer of Kélambakam, shown how this leech in human shape contrives to impoverish the toiling villagers. When the villager's dwelling is to be repaired, to the usurer he must go. If he has to buy a pair of bullocks, he must have recourse to the money-lender. If marriages and other ceremonies are to be performed, the usurer is ever ready to lend him money; and above all, the instalments of Government revenue to be paid before all his crops can be secured and realized, are gladly advanced by the money-lender. The villager can do nothing but borrow at exorbitant rates. Thus, in India, we see the strange anomaly of the money-lender furnishing the cultivator with farming capital. The result is that the poor villager is simply paid for his labour, while the lender takes all the profits, "although he has no proprietary interest in the land." The plant and stock in any concern in which an English capitalist engages belongs to himself, but in India the villager who owns the land is simply in the position of an English labourer, who has no such ownership. And in India we find the still further anomaly of capital without proprietary interest securing a higher rate of interest than that obtainable in England. Here we find the few flourishing while the many suffer. The only remedy is, as I have already pointed out, to institute agricultural banks in every district, and advance money to the cultivators at moderate interest.

Another successful class of people has also sprung up in India. There are to be found in villages nowadays people with a smattering of law leading on innocent people to unnecessary and costly litigation. Every village has its local lawyer, and we have seen how in Kélambakam, Appalacharri successfully managed to bring about a quarrel between the potter and the *panisiva*, how the dispute lingered on for a year and more, how Appalacharri himself played the chief part therein, and how during all that period he successfully fleeced both the parties. The time has now come for steps to be taken to put down this class of men, who are dreaded by the villagers and whose favour is gladly courted by them. A revival of the old system of settling disputes by village *panchayets* would be a step in the right direction.

For the present I take leave of my readers. For years I have freely mingled with the simple villagers, and it is because I feel strongly that they are a people deserving of sympathy that I have ventured to put together these hurried sketches, in the hope that they may lead people to take an interest in their welfare.